Be maker Be happy

Editor, concept, and project director
Anna Minguet

Project's selection, design and layout
Carolina Amell (Monsa Publications)
Cover design
Carolina Amell (Monsa Publications)
Introduction and text edition
Monsa Publications

Cover image by Otter Surfboards
Photo: James and Buddy at the workshop doors
Back cover by Dashing Tweeds

INSTITUTO MONSA DE EDICIONES
Gravina 43 (08930)
Sant Adrià de Besòs
Barcelona (Spain)
Tlf. +34 93 381 00 50
www.monsa.com
monsa@monsa.com

Visit our official online store!
www.monsashop.com

Follow us on facebook!
facebook.com/monsashop

ISBN: 978-84-16500-50-5
D.L. B 9824-2017
Printed by Cachiman

BY CAROLINA AMELL

Be maker be happy

monsa

46.

122.

28.

80.

134.

Intro

From the beginning of time, humans have had the need make things. As small children, we feel such need: we make robots, houses, bridges, dolls, etc. We are born with the desire to create. As Chris Anderson, said "We are all born makers." We can say that the Makers movement can be identified with the DIY culture and the feeling we get when you make something with your bear hands.
Likewise, we can say that said movement is based on hobbies that go from being a leisure activity to an economic force.
The difference between modern Makers and inventors or DIYers from different eras is the power granted by new technology to be connected and learn, as a way to market their creations. Forums, social networks and other sites to publish videos allow the creation of communities and to make questions and collaborate among each other. They share, inspire, and motivate while they transform education, economy and science. The power of the Makers movement knows no limits!

Be Maker Be Happy!

El ser humano desde sus orígenes ha tenido la necesidad de hacer cosas, ya de niños la sentimos, muchas veces hacemos robots, casas, puentes, muñecos, etc. Nacemos con ese deseo de crear "Todos somos *makers* al nacer" dice Chris Anderson. Se puede decir que el movimiento *maker* se identifica con el hágalo-usted-mismo de la cultura DIY, y la sensación de satisfacción que experimentas cuando haces algo con tus propias manos.
Del mismo modo, se podría pensar que el movimiento *maker* está basado esencialmente en los hobbies que han pasado de ser una actividad de recreación, a una nueva fuerza económica.
Lo que distingue a los *makers* contemporáneos de los inventores y los DIYers de otras épocas, es el increíble poder que les brindan las nuevas tecnologías, para conectarse, aprender, y poder comercializar sus creaciones. Foros, redes sociales, y páginas donde publicar sus vídeos, que les permiten formar comunidades, hacer preguntas y colaborar. Comparten, inspiran y motivan, y en el proceso están transformando la educación, la economía y la ciencia.
¡El poder del movimiento *maker* no tiene límites!

Be Maker Be Happy!

88.

94.

52.

22.

68.

Index

IRAN
SAUDI
ARABIA
INDIA
SOMALIA
INDIAN
OCEAN

Bellerby & Co Globemakers

Creators of high quality, beautifully handmade world globes. Combining traditional techniques with modern designs. Handcrafted terrestrial and celestial globes, made in London.

Photos by Alun Callender, Julian Love, Tom Bunning and Ana Santl

A small team of highly trained artists create the high quality, handmade globes that Bellerby & Co. Globemakers have come to be recognised for. From the stand, to the artwork, the painting and map-making, each piece is expertly crafted using both traditional and modern globe-making techniques, and is lovingly produced in their North London studio. Each piece is an individual model of style and grandeur and the larger globes are works of art in their own right.

Bellerby & Co's collection is ever increasing, with the always popular 23cm Mini Desk Globe a favourite as well as the gigantic 127cm Churchill.

Along with the models displayed in their online catalogue, which are all made to order, Bellerby & Co. undertake commissions of all kinds. From personal engravings to personalised maps to hand drawn and hand painted illustrations; a bespoke globe is certainly an excellent way to commemorate a special occasion or a lifetime of adventures.

Un pequeño equipo de artistas con gran formación crean los globos terráqueos de alta calidad hechos a mano por los que Bellerby & Co Globemakers es conocida. Desde el soporte al trabajo artístico, la pintura y la realización de mapas, cada pieza es elaborada, en su estudio del norte de Londres, por manos expertas mediante técnicas tanto tradicionales como modernas y mucho amor. Cada pieza es única tanto por su estilo como su tamaño. Además, los globos más grandes son verdaderas obras de arte.

La colección de Bellerby & Co crece, aunque sigue contando con su popular Mini Desk Globe de 23 cm, así como con la gigante Churchill de 127 cm.

Además de los modelos del catálogo online, todos ellos hechos bajo pedido, Bellerby & Co recibe encargos de todo tipo, desde grabados personalizados hasta mapas a medida con ilustraciones dibujadas y pintadas a mano. Un globo terráqueo personalizado siempre es una excelente forma de conmemorar una ocasión especial o una vida llena de aventuras.

▸ The 36cm Livingstone Desk Globe in Reed Green (Photo by Alun Callender)

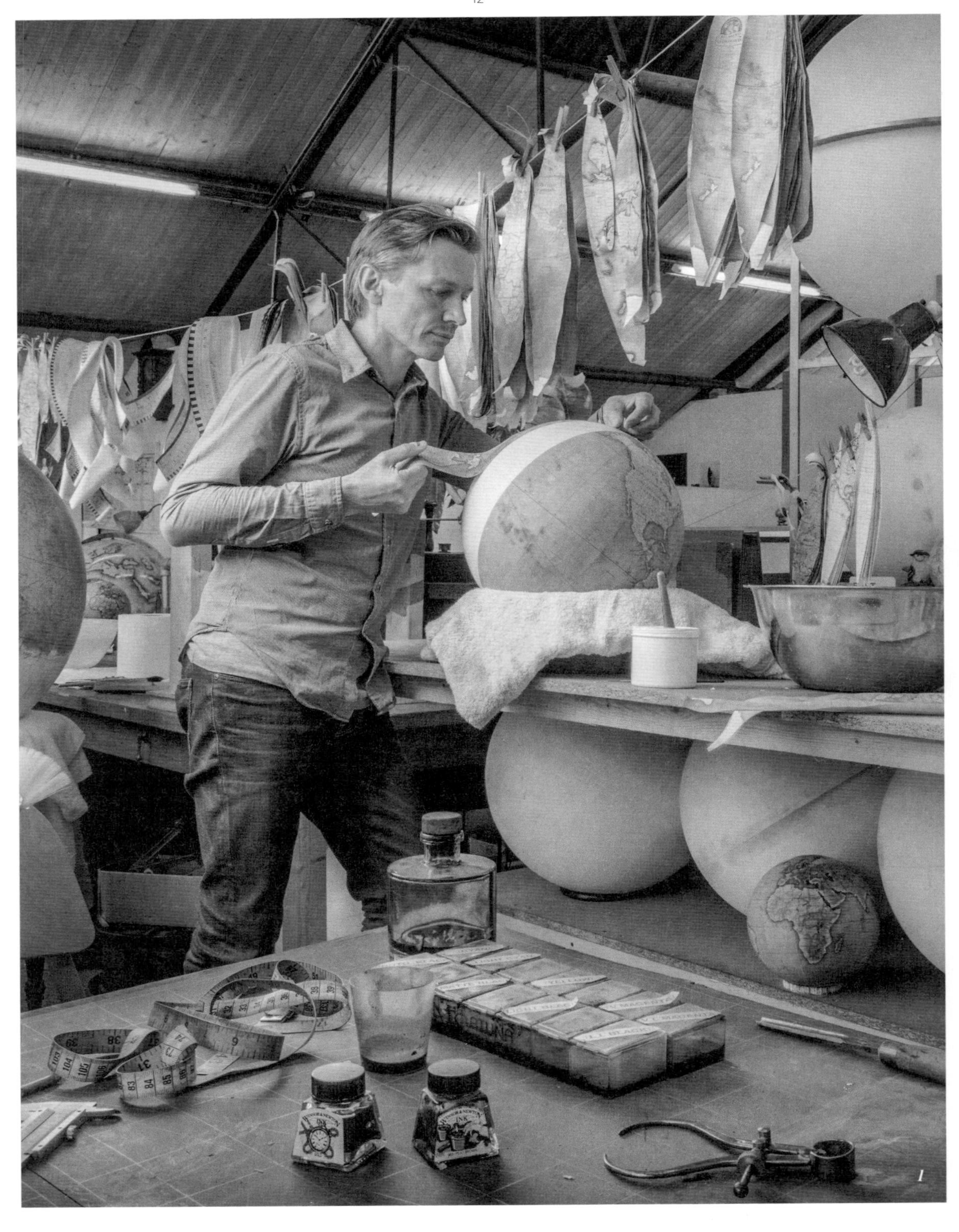

1

Each piece is an individual model of style and grandeur and the larger globes are works of art in their own right.

1. Peter Bellerby laying a gore (Photo by Julian Love) ***2.*** Painting a gore (by Tom Bunning) ***3.*** The studio (by Ana Santl) ***4.*** A Globemaker carefully cutting the a gore (by Ana Santl) ***5.*** Painting the shading around the coast (by Tom Bunning)

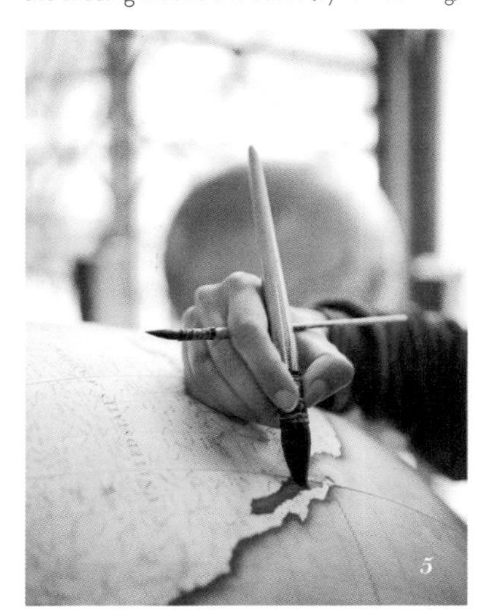

A triumph of craft, skill and precision.

1. A Globemaker at work (Photo by Tom Bunning) *2.* An apprentice (by Andrew Meredith) *3.* An artist paints the ocean of a 127cm Churchill Globe (by Bellerby & Co) *4.* The Studio (by Alun Callender) *5.* An artist paint detail on an 80cm Galileo, a floor standing model (by Gareth Pon) *6.* Gores hang to dry in the studio (by Gareth Pon)

Peter originally wanted to gift a globe to his father for his 80th birthday. After a two year search, he was faced with the choice of a modern plastic factory-made globes, fragile expensive antique models or trying to make his own. He decided to take the adventure. Two years later and after selling his house and car... he finally got it. Today he has his own team of makers: including woodworkers to handcraft the bases, painters of the lands and seas, a fulltime cartographer to ensure the maps are always up to date and skilled artisans to apply the fragile pieces of paper and ensure all the lines match up perfectly without ripping, rippling or overlapping the gores (traingular shaped pieces of the map).

Peter quiso regalar un globo terráqueo a su padre por su 80º cumpleaños. Tras buscar durante dos años, se vio obligado a elegir entre globos de plástico modernos de fabricación mecánica, modelos antiguos frágiles y caros o intentar fabricar su propio globo. Decidió emprender la aventura. Dos años después y tras vender su casa y su coche... por fin lo consiguió. En la actualidad cuenta con un equipo propio de trabajadores entre los que encontramos carpinteros para dar forma a las bases, pintores de tierras y mares, un cartógrafo a jornada completa para garantizar que los mapas siempre están actualizados y habilidosos artesanos que aplican las piezas frágiles de papel y se aseguran de que todas las líneas encajan a la perfección, sin rasgar, plegar o superponer las nesgas (piezas de forma triangular del mapa).

5

6

www.cobblerblack.com

Cuervo Cobblerblack Bird

Cuervo is a little workshop located in Barcelona. We are making classic men and ladies shoes. Some are factory made, some others are entirely hand-made with no machines.

Photos by Alex Castro

Cuervo is a little atelier located in Barcelona in the beginning of Gracia's neighborhood. It is a quiet and very simple place for shoes enthusiasts. The project was started by two shoemakers interested in classic shoes models, those witch have survived over the time.

The most important has always been the shoes by themselves, their construction, the quality of the materials and their simple and elegant pattern and last. At Cuervo you can find a men and women classic ready to wear collection, made with local leathers, great materials, and humble hands.

The atelier, also offers a fine shoeshine service, made by a "maître cireur" who will take care of your beloved shoes with quality creams and waxes.

A selection of accessories and care creams is also available at Cuervo.

Not for fashion victims.

Cuervo es un pequeño taller situado en el barrio barcelonés de Gracia. Se trata de un lugar tranquilo y muy sencillo en el que los entusiastas de los zapatos pueden deleitarse. El proyecto fue iniciado por dos zapateros interesados en los modelos de zapatos clásicos, esos que han sobrevivido al tiempo.

Lo más importante siempre han sido los zapatos en sí, su elaboración, la calidad de los materiales, la sencillez y elegancia de su patrón y su durabilidad. En Cuervo hay colecciones prêt-à-porter clásicas de hombre y de mujer, confeccionadas con pieles locales, excelentes materiales y manos humildes.

El taller cuenta además con un refinado servicio de limpiabotas, ofrecido por un "maître cireur" que cuida sus zapatos más queridos con cremas y ceras de calidad.

Además, Cuervo dispone de una selección de accesorios y cremas de cuidado.

No apto para "fashion victims".

1

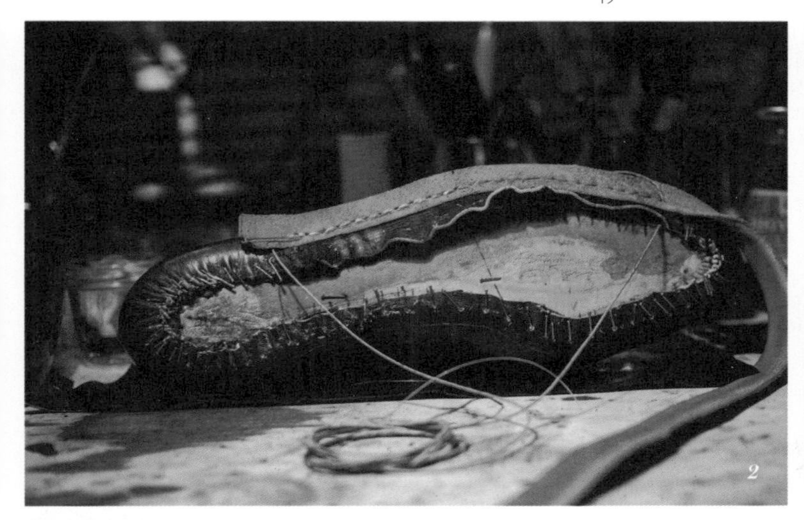

The most important: their construction, the quality of the materials and their simple and elegant pattern and last.

1. Emilio hand welting with awl and linen threads ***2.*** Welt and construction of the shoe on a last ***3.*** Preparing threads and needles ***4.*** Waxing linen threads ***5 and 6.*** Le "maître cireur"

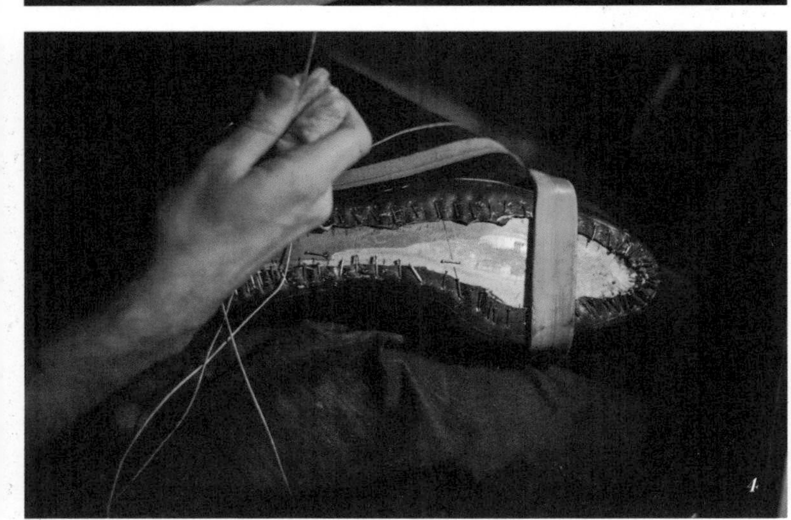

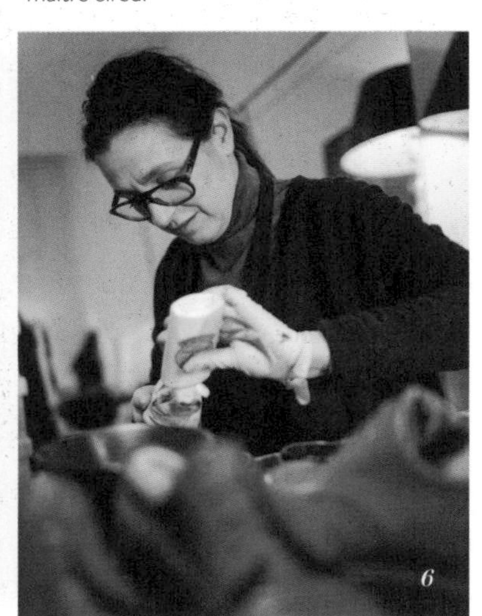

Not for fashion victims.

1, 2 and 3. Classic shoes models
4, 5 and 6. L'atelier

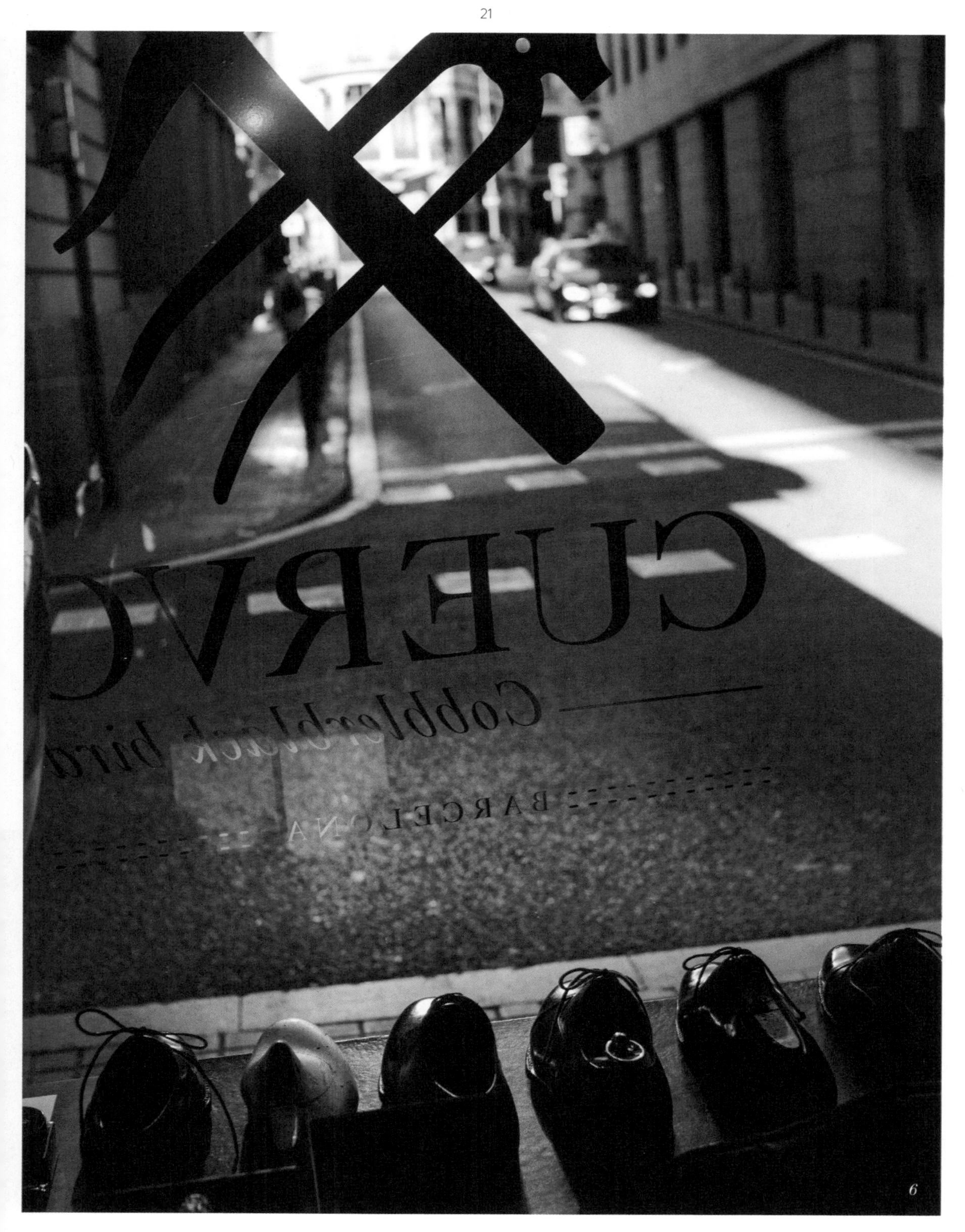

6

Les Catherinettes

A creative space dedicated to all sorts of pieces meant to be worn on the head.

Photos by Andrea Torres Balaguer - Text by Cris Piera

Les Catherinettes is a creative space dedicated to all sorts of pieces meant to be worn on the head. In Gemma's boutique-atelier you'll find some beautiful hats and fascinators, turbans, amazing sculptures designed and crafted with her loving hands and some thrilling treasures from her trips around the world.

As an artisan, Gemma creates her own collections and makes special pieces for well-known designers. Far from serial production, every project is a delicious safari to meet new materials, shapes and structures. In fact, Gemma prefers exploring new territories over using traditional hat-making materials.

Meeting and styling people is also a fascinating part of her life: she studies their features to create custom headpieces or advices them on the best head styling for them, proposes outfits to make the most of their new favourite accessory... "I just love my job, it makes me really happy!"

Les Catherinettes es un espacio creativo dedicado a todo tipo de elementos que puedan llevarse en la cabeza. En la boutique-taller de Gemma encontrará sombreros y tocados preciosos, turbantes y esculturas increíbles, diseñados y elaborados con el cariño de sus manos y tesoros apasionantes de sus viajes por el mundo.

Como artesana, Gemma crea sus propias colecciones y realiza piezas especiales para conocidos diseñadores. Alejados de la producción en serie, cada proyecto es un safari en busca de nuevos materiales, formas y estructuras. De hecho, Gemma prefiere explorar territorios nuevos a utilizar materiales usados tradicionalmente.

Conocer y asesorar al cliente es también una parte fascinante de su vida: estudia sus rasgos para crear piezas personalizadas o les asesora sobre el peinado y ropa mas adecuados para lucir al máximo su nuevo accesorio favorito... "¡Me encanta mi trabajo, me hace realmente feliz!"

▸ Fur felt hats, diferent brands in the store

1

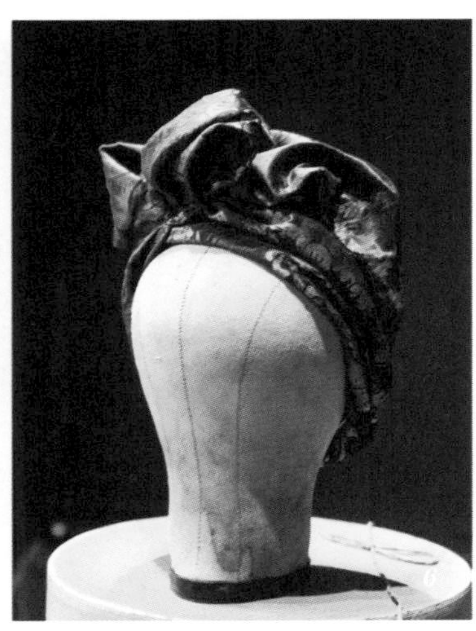

"I just love my job, it makes me really happy!"

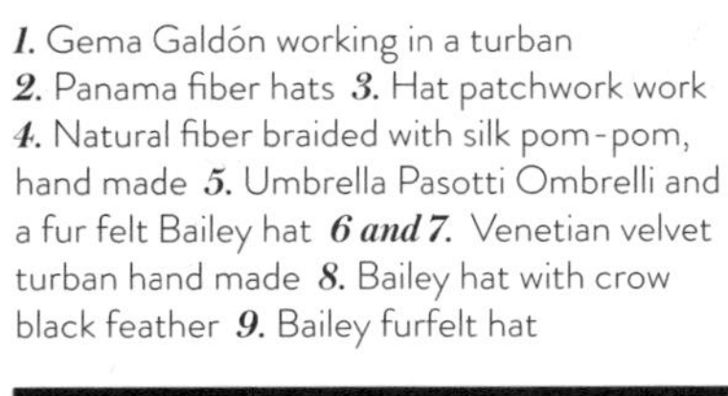

1. Gema Galdón working in a turban *2.* Panama fiber hats *3.* Hat patchwork work *4.* Natural fiber braided with silk pom-pom, hand made *5.* Umbrella Pasotti Ombrelli and a fur felt Bailey hat *6 and 7.* Venetian velvet turban hand made *8.* Bailey hat with crow black feather *9.* Bailey furfelt hat

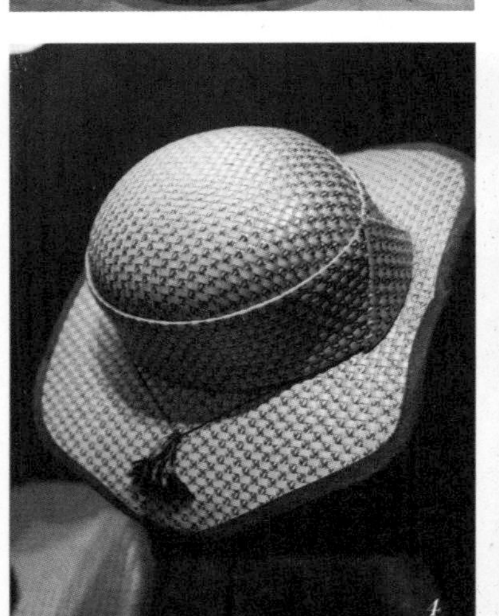

Far from serial production, every project is a delicious safari to meet new materials, shapes and structures.

1. Panama hat with coffee dye and silk bow, artisan process ***2 and 3.*** Natural fiber braided hats and pillow hand made, detail ***4.*** Working process in the workshop ***5.*** Handmade lettering with silver leaf (2 days process for an expert calligrapher) ***6.*** Gema Galdón with maroon cotton velvet turban handmade

6

Flowers by Bornay

"Flowers by Bornay is to floral art what Ferran Adrià is to Gastronomy." This is the beginning of an excerpt from Olivier Dupon's book "Floral Contemporary" on the work of this studio.

Photos by Bornay

Flowers by Bornay was started in 2009 in Barcelona, offering a new, unique iconic universe, daring to break free from the classical conception of the profession to dabble in film culture, science fiction, pop culture, art, dance... and break away from the established norms, using materials and accessories that were previously unthinkable, such as colored spray paint to alter the natural state of the raw materials.

Flowers by Bornay is in charge of the floral decoration for hotels such as the W, Le Meridien and events at the Mandarin Oriental in Barcelona, and has participated in major activities for brands including Hermés, Louis Vuitton, Burberry, Pronovias, Puig, Mango, Zara, Tous, Rolex, and for emblematic spaces and events such as La Pedrera, Casa Batlló, Hospital Sant Pau and Primavera Sound Festival.

Flowers by Bornay empezó en 2009 en Barcelona, imponiendo un nuevo e irrepetible universo icónico, atreviéndose a romper la concepción clásica de la profesión para beber de la cultura del cine, la ciencia ficción, la cultura pop, el arte, la danza... y romper con lo establecido, utilizando materiales y complementos hasta el momento impensables, como el spray de color para alterar el estado natural de la materia prima.

Flowers by Bornay es el responsable de la decoración floral de hoteles como el W, Le Meridien o de los eventos del Mandarin Oriental en Barcelona y ha participado en grandes acciones para marcas como Hermés, Louis Vuitton, Burberry, Pronovias, Puig, Mango, Zara, Tous, Rolex, en espacios y eventos tan emblemáticos como La Pedrera, Casa Batlló, Hospital de Sant Pau o el festival Primavera Sound.

▸ Natural flower bouquet painted with crasas plant

Flowers by Bornay has been recognized twice as one of the best floral art studios in the world by two prestigious international books, including the previously mentioned "Floral Contemporary: The Renaissance in Flower Design" by Olivier Dupon and "Formidable Florists" by Isabel Gilbert Palmer, which referred to the studio as "The Quentin Tarantino of flowers." It has also been named as one of the best floral studios in Spain by the American magazine Martha Stewart Weddings.

Flowers by Bornay ha sido reconocido dos veces como uno de los mejores talleres de arte floral en el mundo por dos libros internacionales de gran prestigio, como son el ya citado "Floral Contemporary: The Renaissance in Flower Design" de Olivier Dupon y el "Formidable Florists" de Isabel Gilbert Palmer en el que se calificó al taller como "El Quentin Tarantino de las flores". Ha sido nombrado también como uno de los mejores talleres florales en España por la revista norteamericana Martha Stewart Weddings.

One of the best floral art studios in the world.

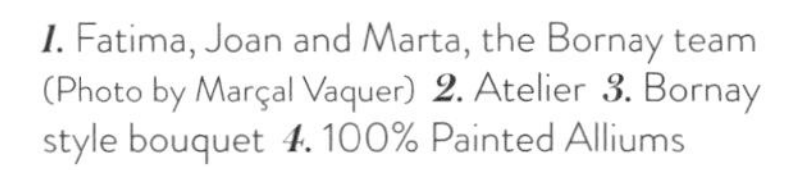

1. Fatima, Joan and Marta, the Bornay team (Photo by Marçal Vaquer) ***2.*** Atelier ***3.*** Bornay style bouquet ***4.*** 100% Painted Alliums

"Our dream: an office with a tree"

1, 2 and 3. Atelier
4. Our tree

Flowers by Bornay breaks free from the classical conception of the profession.

1 and 2. Compositions of artificial painted flower ***3.*** Cactus wall for Hermès (Photo by @irishumm) ***4, 5 and 6.*** Centerpiece with Air Plant

Flowers by Bornay is in charge of the floral decoration for emblematic hotels, space and events.

1. 100% Artificial painted flower ***2.*** Serving customers ***3.*** Centerpiece Bornay style

OTTER
WORKSHOPS

Otter Surfboards

Their surfboards are the product of the shared twin passions of surfing and fine woodworking

Photos by Mat Arney

They make hollow, skin and frame wooden surfboards and share the joy of making them through their workshop courses. Their surfboards are the product of the shared twin passions of surfing and fine woodworking that drive the workshop with a strong nod to the planet that we live on. Wooden surfboards stand separate from the vast majority of petro-chemical derived surfboards found bobbing in line-ups these days; they glide and carry their momentum to help you flow through fat sections, they flex and recoil out of turns in a different and more controlled manner than foam boards, and they look like straight up works of art.

Wood has been a principal material in the construction of surfboards since ancient Hawaiians started to shape wave-riding tools. At Otter Surfboards they look back for inspiration to the construction techniques first pioneered by legendary waterman and surfboard designer Tom Blake in the 1930's, whilst looking forwards towards a future of more considered and harmonious surf craft that enhance enjoyment and accessibility of waves by blending the best of old and new: Traditional materials and techniques with modern refinements and construction methods.

Hacen tablas de surf de madera, huecas y revestidas, y comparten la alegría de hacerlas a través de sus cursos. Sus tablas de surf son el resultado de sus dos pasiones: el surf y la carpintería fina, que les ha llevado a hacer un taller con un enorme respeto por el planeta en el que vivimos. Las tablas de madera se diferencian de la gran mayoría de tablas de derivados petroquímicos, que encontramos hoy en día en el mercado, porque se deslizan y dan impulso para ayudar a fluir a través de secciones grandes, son flexibles y permiten retroceder en los giros de forma diferente y más controlada que las tablas de espuma y además parecen auténticas obras de arte.

La madera ha sido el material principal en la construcción de tablas de surf desde que los antiguos hawaianos comenzaron a fabricar artilugios para navegar sobre las olas. En Otter Surfboards buscan inspiración en las primeras técnicas de construcción utilizadas en los años 30, por el legendario surfista y diseñador de tablas Tom Blake. Buscan mejorar las tablas de forma que permitan disfrutar mas y acceder mas fácilmente a las olas, utilizando la mejor combinación entre lo antiguo y lo nuevo: materiales y técnicas tradicionales con métodos de construcción más sofisticados y modernos.

▸ Cedar, Walnut and poplar surfboard awaiting it's first splash in the sea

1

Wooden surfboards look like straight up works of art.

1. James shaping the tail of a custom surfboard with his low-angle block plane ***2, 3 and 4.*** James working ***5.*** James sanding the rails of a custom surfboard

1

2

3

4

Traditional materials and techniques with modern refinements and construction methods.

1. Boards at variouos stages of completion in the corner of the workshop *2.* James and a very unique surfboard made from English Poplar and reclaimed Californian Redwood *3.* James holding a 5'10 surfboard aloft *4.* James heading into the sea for a few waves *5.* Surfing with Otter surfboard *6.* Marcus glides along a wave on a 7'2 Coaster

5

6

www.glashuettecomploj.at
www.robertcomploj.com

Glashütte Comploj

A master of glass art in Austria.

Photos by Werner Redel

Robert Comploj is a master of glass art. Glashütte Comploj opened in Traun (Upper Austria) in 2013; it is both an exhibition workshop and a gallery.

Robert learned his craft from the world's greatest: the glass blowers of Murano. Robert Comploj draws upon centuries - old knowledge, which he combines with modern design and bold colours. Afterwards he ventured out to spend his learning and wandering years in North America and Denmark. Upon returning to his native Austria he revolutionised the local glassblowing scene - making a name for himself on the way - by introducing new techniques and colours, experimenting with the form and structure of glass and bringing his punk-style approach to the craft.

Robert Comploj es un maestro en el arte del vidrio. Glashütte Comploj se inauguró en Traun (Alta Austria) en 2013 y es tanto taller como galería.

Robert aprendió el oficio de los mejores del mundo, los sopladores de vidrio de Murano. Robert Comploj se basa en conocimientos centenarios, que combina con un diseño moderno y colores atrevidos. Continuó su aprendizaje viajando durante años por América del Norte y Dinamarca. Cuando volvió a su Austria natal, revolucionó la escena local del soplado de vidrio, se hizo un nombre mediante la introducción de nuevas técnicas y colores, experimentando con la forma y estructura del vidrio e introduciendo su estilo punk a un arte tradicional.

▸ Vase Candy Couture

1

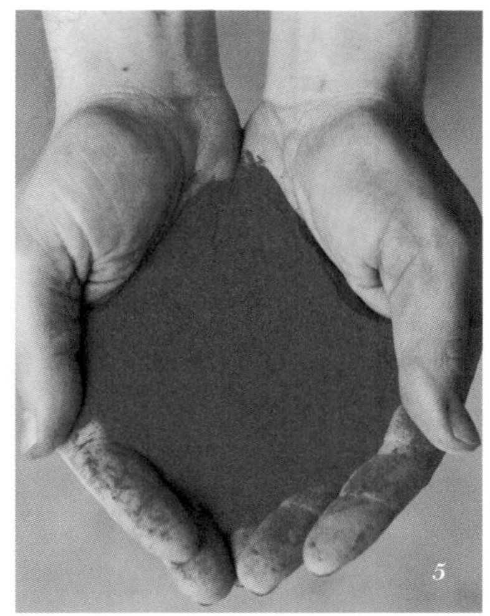

Robert learned his craft from the world's greatest: the glassblowers of Murano.

1. Robert Comploj ***2.*** Making candy couture large ***3.*** Glass Studio in the old Factory in Traun ***4.*** Shaping the hot glass (1000Degrees) with my hand holding just a wet newspaper ***5.*** Coloured glass powder ***6.*** Filigrane for making Venitian Vases

Glashütte Comploj is both an exhibition workshop and a gallery.

1. Vase Roxy ***2.*** Vase Candy Couture
3 and 4. Gallery in our old factory

Robert combines old knowledge with modern design and bold colours.

5. Ornament **6.** Candy Basket **7.** Drinking glass "Imperfect" **8.** Roxy

Nymphenburg manufaktur

In Nymphenburg what it always did, completely handmade, using techniques passed on and preserved from generation to generation.

Photos by Armin Baumgartner, Frank Stolle and Jens Mauritz

Nymphenburg is the porcelain manufactory of the Bavarian crown. The noble art of porcelain-making has been cultivated there since its founding in 1747. Even now, manu factum means in Nymphenburg what it always did, completely handmade, using techniques passed on and preserved from generation to generation. This is the only way to assure the unrivalled fineness, subtlety and brilliance of porcelain that Nymphenburg's global reputation is based on. The manufactory's master workshops produce avantgarde and tailor-made designs from four centuries, created right up to the present day by the most distinguished artists, architects and designers.

The porcelain paste is made on site. Nymphenburg also creates and mixes its own paints; its porcelain painters work without templates. Each item is shaped and painted by hand, each ornament individually applied and all fretwork, be it ever so small, cut with tiny blades into the unfired porcelain. Nymphenburg consciously decided to continue to employ purely manual production methods and, since the 18th century, has refined them almost to perfection.

In Nymphenburg, handmade porcelain objects and works of art are manufactured according to the concepts of contemporary designers and artist who count among some of the most widely-renowned creators of art worldwide.

Nymphenburg es el lugar de fabricación de manufacturas de porcelana de la corona de Baviera. El noble arte de la elaboración de porcelana se ha cultivado aquí desde 1747. Actualmente, manu factum mantiene en Nymphenburg el significado original, fabricado totalmente a mano, utilizando técnicas que han pasado y se han conservado generación tras generación. El único modo de garantizar el refinamiento, sutileza y brillo de la porcelana que otorgan a Nymphenburg fama mundial. En sus talleres las manos de los mejores artistas, arquitectos y diseñadores han elaborado diseños innovadores y a medida durante cuatro siglos y hasta la actualidad.

La masa de la porcelana se realiza *in situ*. Nymphenburg crea y mezcla además sus propias pinturas, y sus pintores trabajan sin plantillas. Cada elemento se forma y pinta a mano, cada ornamento se aplica de manera individual y la totalidad del calado, por pequeño que sea, se corta con cuchillas diminutas en la porcelana cruda. Nymphenburg decidió continuar empleando métodos de producción puramente manuales y, desde el siglo XVIII, los ha refinado casi a la perfección.

En Nymphenburg, los objetos de porcelana y obras de arte realizados se fabrican conforme a los conceptos de diseñadores y artistas contemporáneos, entre los que se encuentran algunos conocidos a nivel mundial.

33
SPORTY

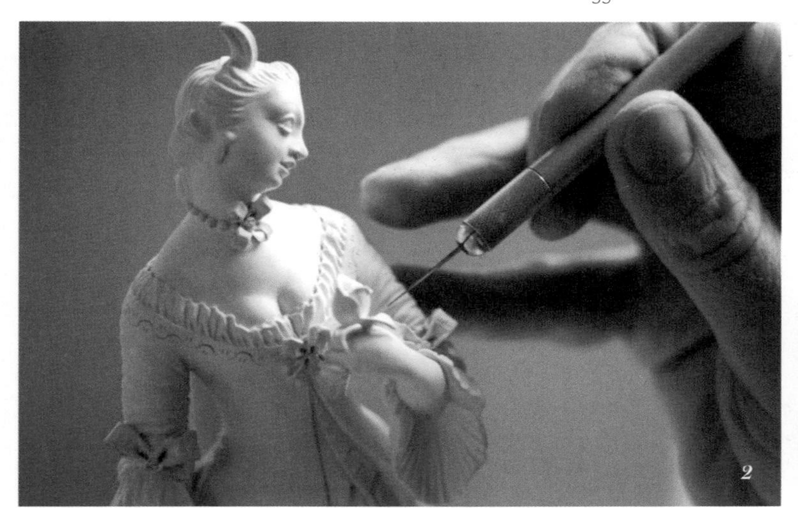

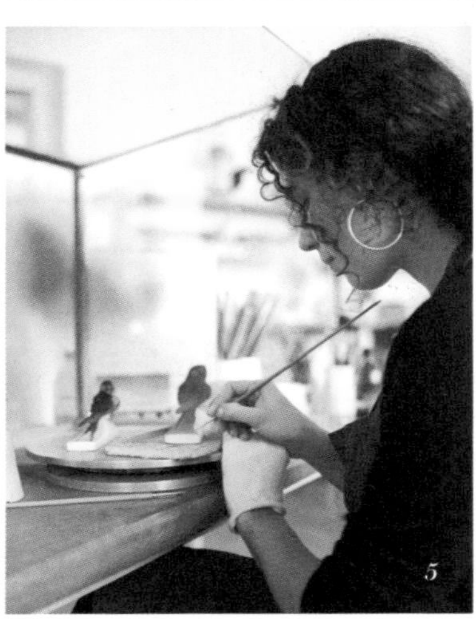

The porcelain paste is made on site. They also create and mix its own paints.

1. Dieter Zeus in the paste mill ***2.*** The modellers work out plastic details as hands ***3.*** The model shop ***4.*** The turning shop ***5.*** In underglaze painting, the paint is brushed or sprayed before their first glazing

Nymphenburg aims to consistently face up the challenges of the 21st century and create outstanding works of art with timeless values.

1. One of the exclusive rooms in the Nymphenburg Palais is dedicated to figures ***2.*** Turning shop ***3.*** Moulds in the model shop

All are made by hand on potter's wheels

4. The contemporary room with pieces by Ruth Gurvich and Ted Muehling
5. Rhinoceros "Clara", a hare and a lying stag in white biscuit porcelain ***6.*** Lotos aqua plates

Dashing Tweeds

Guy and Kirsty set up their weave design studio in East London, using the best mills in the country.

Photos by Guy Hills

Successful fashion photographer Guy Hills launched British brand Dashing Tweeds in 2006 with the talented head of Woven Textiles at the Royal College of Art, Kirsty McDougall.

Guy was looking to create a British high quality modern tweed that could be worn in the city.

His passion was to combine traditional sportswear with new designs and technical yarns.

Guy and Kirsty set up their weave design studio in East London, using the best mills in the country to create high luxury woven designs.

With the cloth's instant success amongst Savile Row tailors, the Dashing Tweeds Flagship store opened in 2014 in Mayfair, London.

Today, Dashing Tweeds produce two seasonal fabric collections a year alongside their newly launched ready to wear menswear line, first seen at London Collections Men for AW16.

El exitoso fotógrafo de moda Guy Hills lanzó la marca británica Dashing Tweeds en 2006 junto a la talentosa Kirsty McDougall, directora de Woven Textiles en la Royal College of Art.

Guy quería crear un tweed moderno, británico y de alta calidad que pudiera utilizarse en la ciudad.

Su pasión era combinar ropa de sport tradicional con diseños nuevos e hilos técnicos.

Guy y Kirsty abrieron su estudio de diseño de tejidos en el este de Londres, recurriendo a las mejores fábricas del país para crear diseños tejidos de lujo.

Gracias al éxito inmediato de su tejido entre los sastres de Savile Row, en 2014 la tienda Dashing Tweeds Flagship abrió sus puertas en Mayfair, Londres.

En la actualidad, Dashing Tweeds elabora dos colecciones temporales de tejidos al año, junto a su nueva línea de ropa para hombre, presentada en la London Collections Men para la temporada Otoño-Invierno 2016.

▸ Guy Hills in the original Dashing design

Once again colour and texture have been brought back to the forefront of men's fashion and with this Dashing Tweeds is modernising traditional tweed fabrics, bringing colour, creativity and innovation to the urban environment. Traditional designs are being updated and entirely new original weave structures are being created.

Dashing Tweeds only work with the highest quality yarns and most technically experienced mills in the country as British heritage is very important to the brand. Whilst both British and fine Merino wools are combined with advanced yarns from around the world, all their cloth is woven in Britain.

Una vez más el color y las texturas vuelven a la vanguardia de la moda para hombre y vemos a Dashing Tweeds modernizando el tweed tradicional y aportando color, creatividad e innovación al entorno urbano. Los diseños tradicionales se han actualizado y se han creado estructuras tejidas originales y totalmente nuevas.

Dashing Tweeds sólo trabaja con hilos de la mejor calidad y fábricas con la mayor experiencia técnica del país, ya que la herencia británica resulta fundamental para la marca. Aunque se combinan lanas británicas y finas lanas merino con avanzados hilos de todo el mundo, todas sus piezas se tejen en Gran Bretaña.

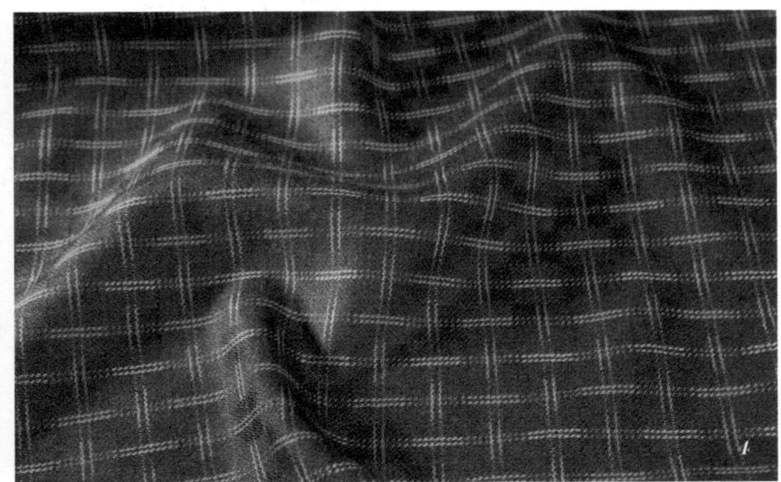

Dashing Tweeds creates high luxury woven designs.

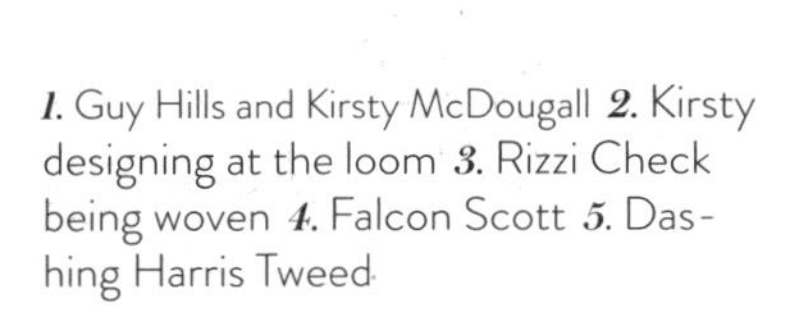

1. Guy Hills and Kirsty McDougall *2.* Kirsty designing at the loom *3.* Rizzi Check being woven *4.* Falcon Scott *5.* Dashing Harris Tweed

Dashing Tweeds is modernising traditional tweed fabrics.

1. Emmanuel wearing a Lumatwil Cap by Karen Henriksen and a suit by Davies and Sons ***2.*** Our Shop at 26 Sackville Street London W1S 3HE ***3.*** Shop interior

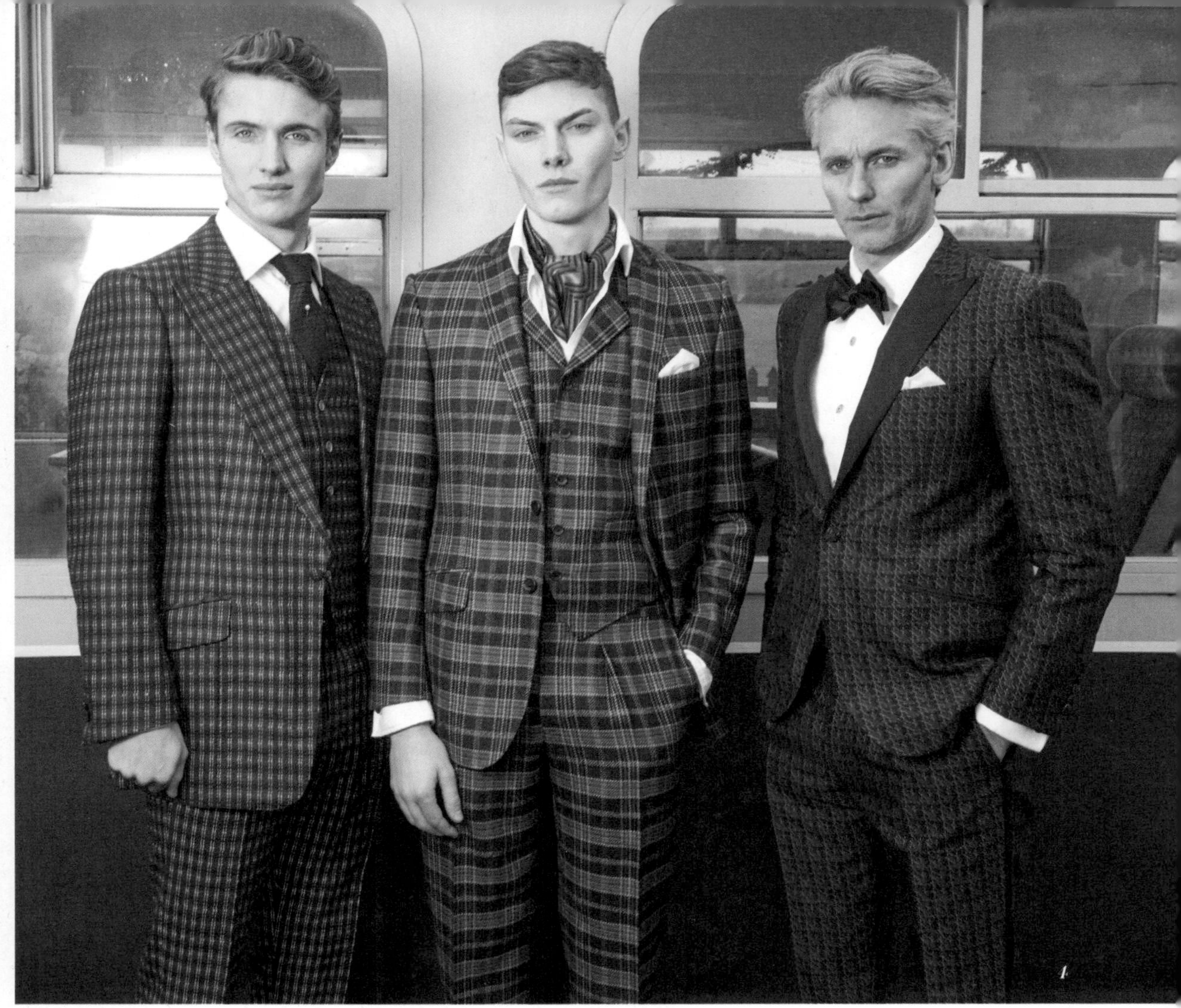

Colour and texture have been brought back to the forefront of men's fashion.

4. Our AW17 Catwalk Video shoot featuring L to R Navy Lumatwill Suit, Rizzi Check Suit and Exploded Houndstooth dinner suit *5.* Detail of our Shetland Jig design *6.* Detail of our Fisher design

Traditional designs are being updated and entirely new original weave structures are being created.

1. Guy Hills with our tweed stock
2. Ian Bruce in the Centre Point suit
3. Navy Raver Lumatwill suit *4.* Pea Coat in Green Whizz *5.* Shoes in Red Route Herringbone by Crockett and Jones

Tom Raffield

Tom Raffield transforms solid wood into sculptural pieces of art.

Photos by Tom Raffield

Renowned for his innovative steam bending techniques, furniture and lighting designer Tom Raffield transforms solid wood into sculptural pieces of art. With an experimental workshop set among six acres of ancient woodland in Cornwall, England, his designs take inspiration from the natural environment that surrounds him.

"Steam bending is an ancient art form traditionally associated with boat building, but I'm forever fascinated with the endless possibilities of steam bent wood. Each piece we create has been on an experimental journey - individual, organic and carefully considered. We source everything we can from sustainably managed woodlands forests, and coupled with the low-energy steam bending process, it's very ecological with little wastage," explains Tom.

"I truly believe that sustainability should be synonymous with good design - much like quality and function are - and this is a crucial part of our design philosophy at Tom Raffield."

Conocido por sus innovadoras técnicas de curvado con vapor, el diseñador de mobiliario y elementos de iluminación Tom Raffield transforma simples piezas de madera en esculturales obras de arte. Con un taller experimental situado en medio de dos hectáreas de antiguos bosques de Cornwall (Inglaterra), sus diseños se inspiran en el entorno natural que le rodea.

"El curvado con vapor es una forma de arte ancestral asociada tradicionalmente con la construcción de barcos, pero a mí siempre me han fascinado las infinitas posibilidades de la madera curvada con vapor. Cada pieza que creamos, ha recorrido un viaje experimental, individual, orgánico y cuidadoso. Obtenemos todo lo que podemos de zonas boscosas gestionadas de manera sostenible para combinarlo con un proceso de curvado con vapor de baja energía, implementando así métodos muy ecológicos que generan muy poca cantidad de residuos", explica Tom.

"Creo realmente que la sostenibilidad debería ser sinónimo de buen diseño, igual que lo son la calidad y funcionalidad, se trata de un elemento fundamental de nuestra filosofía de diseño en Tom Raffield."

▸ Amble Hanging Seat

1

"I truly believe that sustainability should be synonymous with good design."

1. Tom Raffield *2.* Inspired by nature *3.* Quality craftsmanship *4.* Making the No.1 Pendant *5.* Shaped by steam *6.* Manipulating timber into shape

Steam bending is an ancient art form traditionally associated with boat building.

1. Coat Loop ***2.*** Butterfly Pendant and Treave Dining Table ***3.*** Arbor Armchair and Archer Table Light ***4.*** Arbor Armchair ***5.*** May Coffee Table

His designs take inspiration from the natural environment that surrounds him.

6. Skipper Pendant ***7.*** Urchin Wall Light ***8.*** Log Loop ***9.*** Urchin Pendant ***10.*** Skipper Pendant

www.chiaragrifantini.com

Chiara Grifantini

Hand painted textile.

Photos by Silvia Tenenti

Chiara worked for several years as a set designer for a number of Italian an French films makers. She travelled and lived in Australia, New Zealand and the US, searching manual crafts and decorative arts from the Aboriginal, Maori and Native American cultures. She studied to the history of English textile design.

Chiara craft using natural materials; largely raw silk, linen and cotton on which she hand-paints to produce bespoke fabric. Designs are derived from her own pencil and ink drawings or from ideas and patterns provided by her clients. Her signature style is heavily influenced by her passion of the details within nature: plants, insects, cloud formations, etc. And just like nature itself, each of her creations is completely unique; the inevitable imprefections being the salt of finished product.

Chiara trabajó durante años como escenógrafa para numerosos realizadores cinematográficos italianos y franceses. Posteriormente viajó y vivió en Australia, Nueva Zelanda y EE.UU., en busca de oficios manuales y artes decorativas aborígenes, maorís y de culturas nativas americanas. También estudió historia del diseño textil inglés.

Chiara trabaja con materiales naturales, seda, lino y algodón bruto en los que pinta a mano para crear telas personalizadas. Los diseños se basan tanto en dibujos a lápiz y tinta propios como en ideas y patrones sugeridos por sus clientes. Su estilo se ve muy influenciado por su pasión por los detalles de la naturaleza: plantas, insectos, formaciones de nubes, etc. Y como ocurre con la naturaleza, cada una de sus creaciones es totalmente única; las imperfecciones inevitables son la sal del producto acabado.

▸ Fabric detail

"There is something about handcrafted products: every piece has an individual flavour."

1. Chiara Grifantini *2.* Working on a Deco Collection fabric *3.* Sample fabric *4.* Atelier/studio *5.* Working on the Hydrangea Wall Hanging Collection Hand Painted on linen

Chiara has learned from manual crafts and decorative arts from the Aboriginal, Maori and Native American cultures.

1. Hand Painted samples fabric *2.* Botany Collection Hand Painted cushion on linen *3.* Botany & Dragonly Collection *4.* Wall Hanging Botany Collection detail on raw silk

"I am an instictive artist and my trend is the spontaneus expression of the fantasy."

5 and 6. Golden Mermaid Collection sample ***7.*** Golden Dragonfly Collection ***8 and 9.*** Botany & Dragonfly Wall Hanging Collection painted on linen

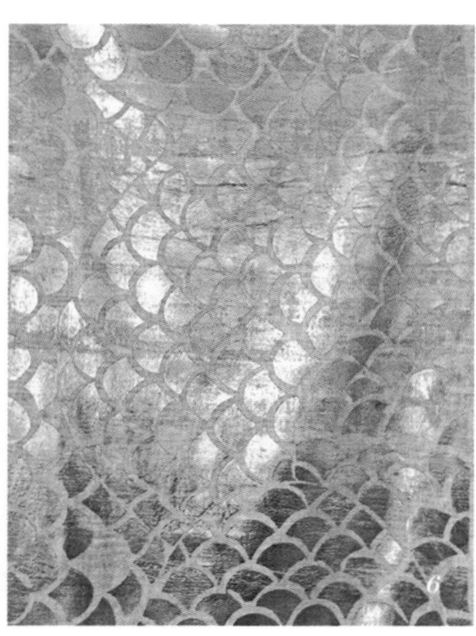

www.feinedinge.at

Feinedinge

Feinedinge* is specialized in developing and producing sustainable porcelain design with high use value.

Photos by Wolfgang Zlodej, Robert Marksteiner and Wolfgang Silveri

Feinedinge* is an Austrian/Vienna based product design label founded in 2005 by Sandra Haischberger. The company is specialized in developing and producing sustainable porcelain design with high use value.

The material porcelain is supposed to be touched and felt. The mixture of handicraft and tradition is essential. Qualities from the past and the present are assembled. Drawing all its secrets from the material is exactly the challenge. Experimenting and testing are greatest passions anyway.

The products combine textured surfaces and delicate structures on the exterior of the objects. With the latest collection "Alice", colour is tinted through the porcelain clay to provide a colour depth not available from surface glazing. Clear glaze is then applied to the interior of each piece leaving the exterior with a vitrified stone-like surface, which becomes smooth with handling.

The functional design and colour of the range gives the products great flexibility and allows them to be combined in many different ways.

Each piece is entirely hand made in their Viennese studio which makes each a completely unique design item.

Feinedinge* es una etiqueta de diseño de productos con sede en Viena (Austria), fundada en 2005 por Sandra Haischberger. La compañía está especializada en el desarrollo y elaboración de diseños sostenibles en porcelana, con gran valor de uso.

La porcelana se debe tocar y sentir. La combinación de artesanía y tradición es esencial. Las cualidades del pasado y el presente se unen. Extraer todos los secretos del material es precisamente el desafío. Experimentar y probar son las principales pasiones.

Los productos combinan superficies con texturas y estructuras delicadas en su exterior. En su última colección, "Alice", el color se introduce en la masa de porcelana para proporcionar una profundidad no presente con el esmaltado de superficie. Y luego se aplica un esmalte claro al interior de cada pieza, dejando el exterior con una superficie vidriada similar a la piedra que se suaviza con el trabajo manual.

El diseño funcional y el color de la gama proporcionan a los productos gran flexibilidad y permite combinarlos de muchas maneras diferentes.

Todas las piezas se hacen a mano en el estudio de Viena, lo que las convierte en elementos de diseño únicos.

▸ Ceramics (Photo by Wolfgang Zlodej)

For Sandra Haischberger, there are a few things that she would call her working principles; and she woudn`t deviate from them even for a lot of money. The mixture of handicraft and tradition is essential for her work, tailored to fit her style and translated into her own unique language of design. She would never want to exchange the nature of her manufacture for serial mass production; her products are meant to be used and not to become museum pieces.

Los principios básicos del trabajo de Sandra Haischberger son pocos pero nunca se desviaría de ellos, ni siquiera por una gran cantidad de dinero. La combinación de artesanía manual y tradición, adaptada a su estilo y traducida en un idioma de diseño propio, es esencial en su trabajo. Nunca cambiaría la naturaleza de su fabricación por una producción masiva en serie. Sus productos están hechos para ser usados, no para a convertirse en piezas de museo.

Experimenting and testing are Sandra greatest passions.

1. Sandra Haischberger ***2.*** Retouching ***3.*** Glazing ***4.*** Sandra at her studio

The range consists of tableware, home accessories and light objects.

1, 2 and 3. ALICE tea & dining (Photo by Wolfgang Silveri)

Feinedinge* products are made with love, sustainable, beautiful!

4 and 5. raw porcelain; made from recycled porcelain mass (Photo by Wolfgang Zlodej)
6, 7 and 8. pure/iVY bowls (by Robert Marksteiner)

KLINGELN

www.irishantverk.se

Iris Hantverk

Brushes that give "Hand-Made" a new meaning

Photos by Anna Kern

In the late 1900s century a small brush manufacturing started out in Stockholm. It was a successful movement so successful that it remains today. Now, as then, every brush is made by hand by visually impaired craftsmen. It brings new dimensions to the concept of sensitively made by hand. They focus on functional design an carefully selected natural materials. Combined with their expert craftsmanship, this gives every brush a unique function.

All brushes are of exclusive design and made mostly from natural materials.

A finales del siglo XX, una pequeña fábrica de cepillos abrió sus puertas en Estocolmo. Tuvo tanto éxito que aún sigue existiendo. En la actualidad, al igual que por aquel entonces, los cepillos estan hechos a mano por artesanos con discapacidad visual. Esto añade nuevas dimensiones al concepto de realización sensible a mano. Se focaliza en un diseño funcional y el uso de materiales naturales cuidadosamente seleccionados. Combinados con una artesanía experta, cada cepillo presenta una función única.

Todos los cepillos cuentan con un diseño exclusivo y están fabricados con materiales naturales.

▸ Dust brush in light goat hair and broom in horse hair

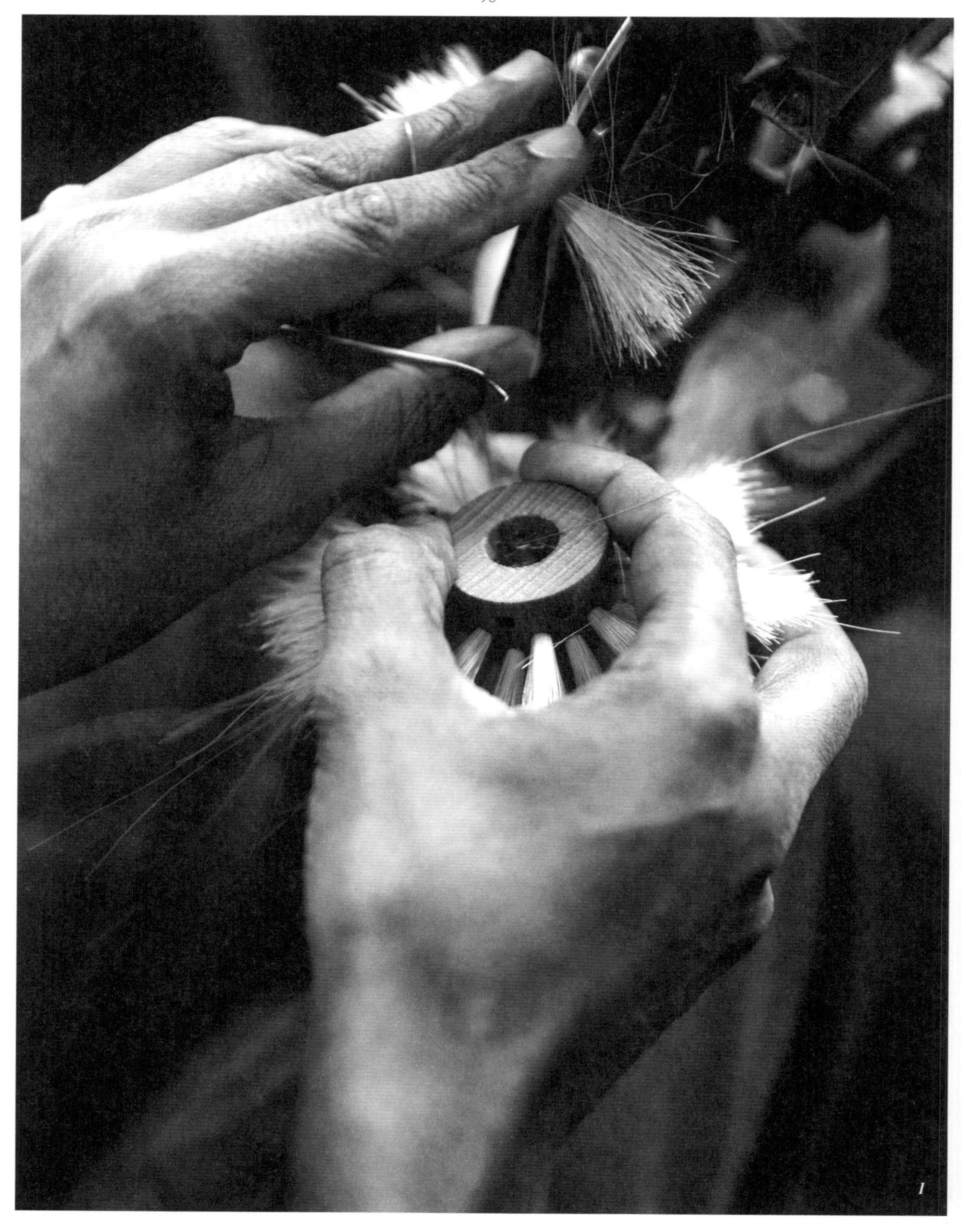
1

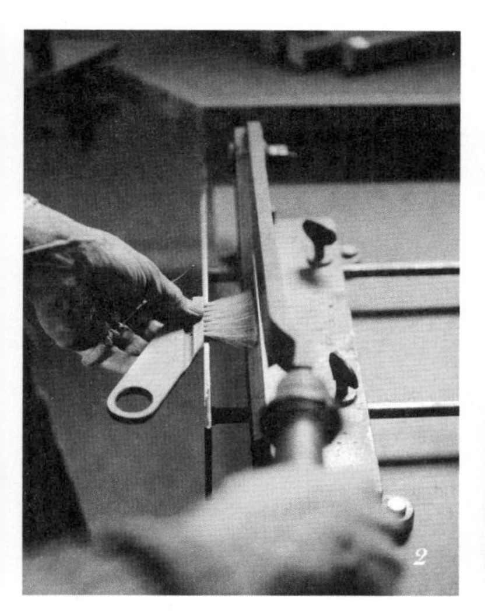

"Our brushes have been carefully designed with a purpose in mind; they're made made to last." Sara Edhäll.

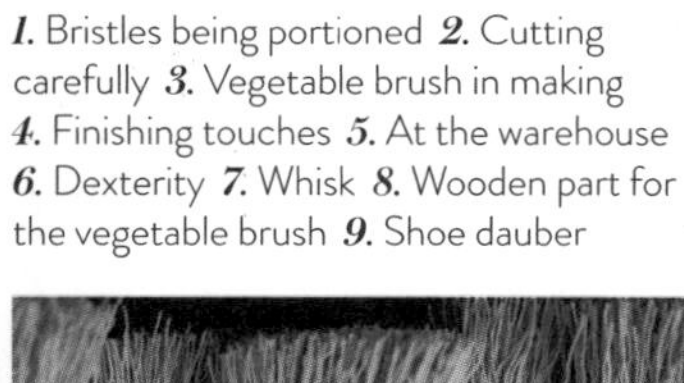

1. Bristles being portioned ***2.*** Cutting carefully ***3.*** Vegetable brush in making ***4.*** Finishing touches ***5.*** At the warehouse ***6.*** Dexterity ***7.*** Whisk ***8.*** Wooden part for the vegetable brush ***9.*** Shoe dauber

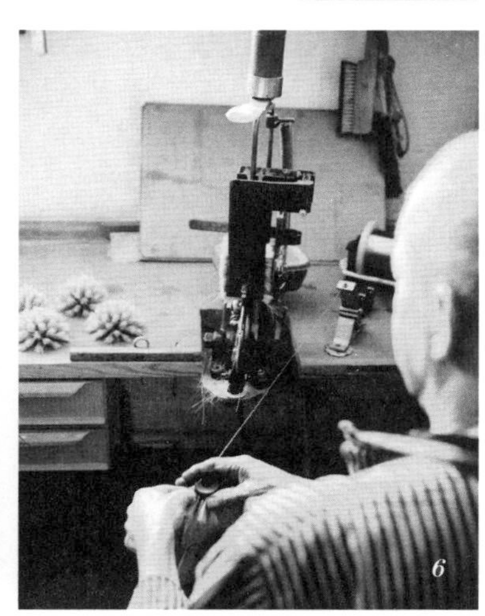

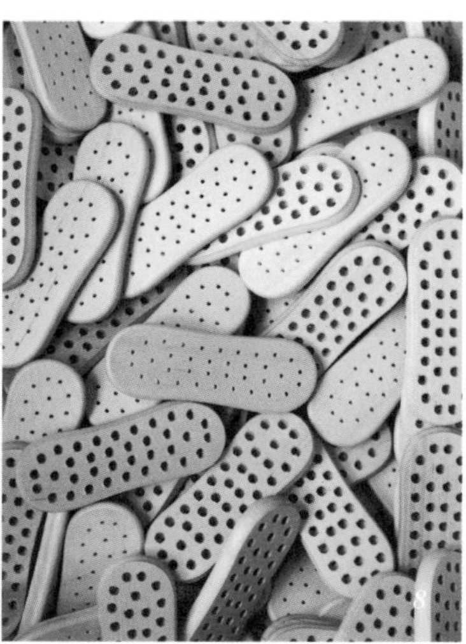

Design has evolved through the years but the craftsmen still use the same time honoring techniques used for over a hundred years.

1. Dustpan & brushset *2.* Bathbrushes at Iris Hantverks store *3.* Iris Hantverk store *4.* Bathbrushes

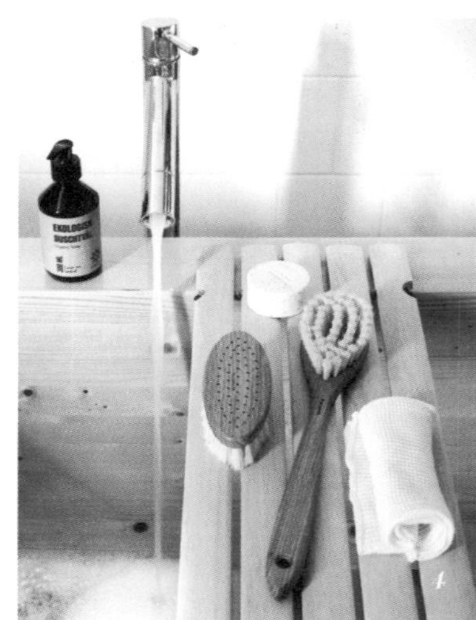

Every brush has a unique function.

5. Bathbrushes *6.* Cleaning attire at it's best
7. Kitchen items *8.* Bathroom inspiration
9. Brushes and towels in eco-cotton

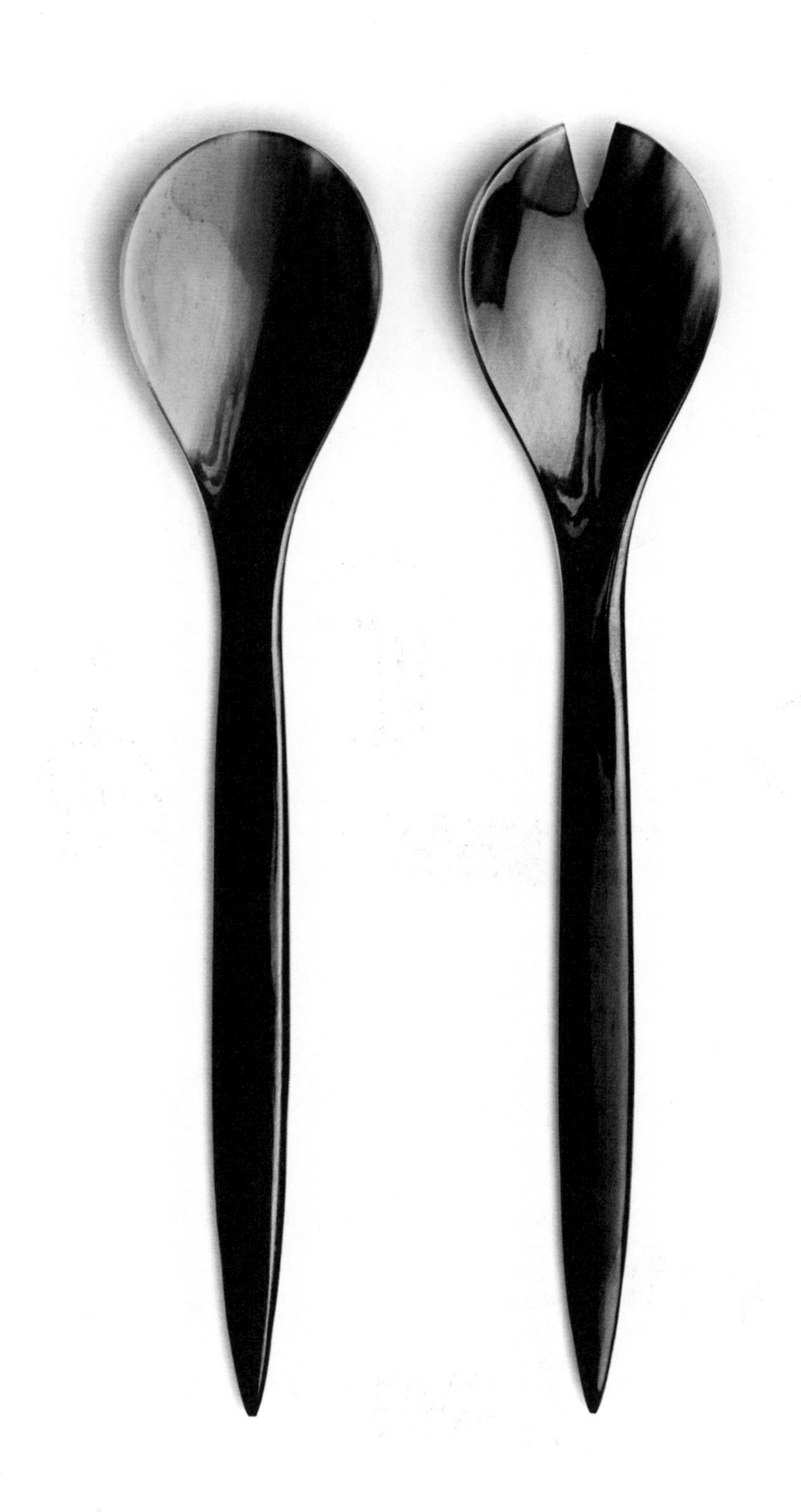

Hornvare-fabrikken

Their ongoing objective it to preserve and renew the craft so it will be kept alive for many generations to come.

Their core principle is simple: "We do not wish to be the world's largest company, but strive to be the absolute best in manufacturing and retailing handmade crafts of horn of impeccable quality". Their founder Peter Husted laid out the ground work by winning a silver medal for his work at the 1935 Brussels World Fair. An awe-inspiring achievement, that set the standards for successors to come. The methods involved in creating the goods, have not changed much over the years. The craftsmanship still requires a great amount of attention to detail and skillful handling of heavy machinery that for some part date back to the 1920s. Today they merely see themselves as a link between the past and the future, with an ongoing objective to preserve and renew the craft so it will be kept alive for many generations to come.

In this quest, they devote a lot of their resources into pursuing perfection at the part of their business that interacts with the end-consumer. Their belief is that the magic happens in the human to human interaction and that every customer must be embraced with kindness and warmth. Today their product can be experienced in their own three contemporary stores in Bøvlingbjerg, Aarhus and Flensburg and at retailers in 25 different countries across the globe.

Su principio fundamental es sencillo: "No queremos ser la compañía más grande del mundo, sino que nos esforzamos para convertirnos en los mejores en la fabricación y venta de objetos de cuerno hechos a mano y de una calidad exquisita." Su fundador, Peter Husted, despegó tras ganar una medalla de plata por su trabajo en la Feria Mundial de Bruselas de 1935. Un impresionante logro que estableció las bases a sus sucesores. Los métodos utilizados no han cambiado demasiado a lo largo de los años. Sigue requiriendo gran atención por el detalle y un hábil manejo de maquinaria pesada, algunas de las piezas de dicha maquinaria son de los años 20. En la actualidad, se consideran un mero vínculo entre el pasado y el futuro, con el objetivo continuado de conservar y renovar el oficio para que siga vivo generación tras generación.

En esta misión, dedican muchos de sus recursos a lograr la perfección en la parte del negocio asociada a la interacción con el consumidor final. Creen que la magia surge en la interacción humano con humano, por lo que se debe abrazar a cada cliente con amabilidad y aprecio. Hoy en día, encontramos sus productos en sus tres modernas tiendas de Bøvlingbjerg, Aarhus y Flensburg y en establecimientos de 25 países diferentes de todo el mundo.

▸ Two spoons

1

The methods involved in creating the goods, have not changed much over the years.

1. The owners: Sara & Peder Buch *2.* The employees: Per, Rasmus, Peder, Sara, Lise, Alina, Maren & Anette *3.* Sanding *4.* Per working at the bandsaw from 1920 *5.* Drawing the final shape *6.* Spoons before polishing

"We devote a lot of our resources into pursuing perfection."

1. The shop ***2.*** Tableware on display
3. Marmelade with spoon

Handmade crafts of horn of impeccable quality.

from 4 to 11. Selection of our products

www.bonfieldblockprinters.com

Bonfield Block-Printers

The tools: a wonderful hand-cranked press from 1904.

Photos by Cameron Short

They are Cameron Short and Janet Tristram, husband and wife and founders of 'Bonfield Block-Printers'.

Home is a crooked Georgian house, complete with its own shop, in a corner of West Dorset, England. Surrounded by woods, ancient hill forts and ramshackle farms, and with Lyme Bay not far away, they find inspiration in every direction. Their work is rooted in their love of both the countryside and sea, rural life - its rhythms and traditional skills - and the folklore of trees, plants and animals. It is often created in repeat, and has a strong narrative element. The tools which give their imagery life are their carving gouges and scoops, and a wonderful hand-cranked press from 1904. Their workshop is the old Thorncombe village stores, still with its handsome original frontage and timber-lined interior. Inside, you'll glimpse their printing paraphernalia (including their blocks) and be able to peruse, and buy, their wares. Their block-printed products include limited edition prints on paper, greetings cards, cushions, lampshades, one-off pieces of furniture and small runs of textile. They hope to offer wallpaper soon. They also undertake illustration and branding/logo design commissions, as well as running block-printing day workshops for groups of up to three people.

Ellos son Cameron Short y Janet Tristram, marido y mujer, y fundadores de 'Bonfield Block-Printers'.

Su casa es un edificio georgiano, con tienda propia, situada en West Dorset, Inglaterra. Rodeada de bosques, antiguos castros y granjas desvencijadas, no lejos de Lyme Bay, encuentran inspiración en cualquier dirección. Su trabajo se basa en su amor tanto por el entorno rural como por el mar, sus ritmos y capacidades tradicionales, el folclore de los árboles, las plantas y los animales. A menudo la repetición es un gran elemento narrativo. Las herramientas utilizadas para dar vida a sus imaginería son sus gubias y palas de tallar, unidas a una maravillosa prensa manual de 1904. Su taller se encuentra en los antiguos comercios de la localidad de Thorncombe y aún cuenta con una preciosa fachada y un interior de madera originales. Dentro, observamos toda su parafernalia de impresión (incluidos sus bloques) y podemos ver y comprar sus productos. Entre sus productos encontramos impresiones de edición limitada en papel, tarjetas de felicitación, cojines, tulipas, piezas de mobiliario únicas y pequeñas piezas de textiles. Esperan poder ofrecer también papeles pintados. Asimismo, aceptan encargos de diseño de logotipos/elementos de marca e ilustraciones, además de impartir talleres sobre impresión de bloque para grupos de un máximo de tres personas.

▸ 'Ode to the Ash' chair

Their work is rooted in their love of both the countryside and sea.

1. Cameron and Janet ***2.*** Cameron at the press ***3.*** 'Treasure Tree' (detail) carved block ***4.*** 'Bloodlines' block print on fine linen ***5.*** Inked block awaits printing

Their workshop is the old Thorncombe village stores, still with its handsome original frontage.

1. Bonfield Block-Printers, Dorset, England
2. 'Varx' block-printed linen lampshade
3. 'Nightjars' block-printed linen lampshade
4. Original shelving in the atelier

SAMSON

www.bobjohnstonbaskets.co.uk

Bob Johnston

Bob creates bespoke, contemporary showpiece willow animal sculptures which are both lifesize and realistic.

Photos by Cristian Barnett

Based in Bangor, County Down, Bob Johnston has been weaving with willow since 2000. Initially trained as a textile weaver, Bob has since studied with master basket makers in Armagh, Galway and Villaines les Rochers, France.

Bob creates bespoke, contemporary showpiece willow animal sculptures which are both lifesize and realistic. Inspired by Victorian trophy heads, each piece is woven by hand and completely unique.

Bob grows over 40 different varieties of willow to enable him to choose from a large palette of colours and textures. Each rod is carefully selected and used in a dense, random weave creating form with detail, giving a feeling of movement and injecting a hint of expression.

His award winning work can be found in the collections of museums, galleries and in the film industry.

Afincado en Bangor, County Down, Bob Johnston ha tejido con sauce desde el año 2000. Con formación inicial como tejedor de textiles, Bob estudió posteriormente junto a maestros cesteros de Armagh, Galway y Villaines les Rochers (Francia).

Bob crea esculturas contemporáneas con sauce, son esculturas de animales y de gran realismo. Inspiradas en las cabezas trofeo victorianas, cada pieza se teje a mano y es completamente única.

Bob cultiva más de 40 variedades de sauce para poder elegir entre una gran paleta de colores y texturas. Cada vara se selecciona cuidadosamente y se utiliza como parte de un tejido denso y aleatorio, logrando sensación de movimiento e inyectando un toque de expresión.

Su premiado trabajo puede encontrarse en colecciones de museos, galerías y en la industria del cine.

▸ Highland Cow head under construction

1

Bob grows over 40 different varieties of willow.

1. Bob Johnston ***2.*** Willow rods soaked to render pliable ***3, 4 and 6.*** Individual willow rods selected and woven ***5.*** Traditional hand tools, Shop knives,wrapping iron, grease horn and bodkin

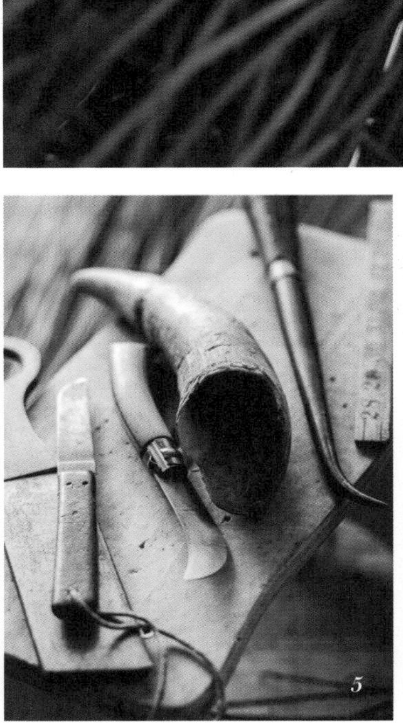

Each piece is woven by hand and completely unique.

1. Stag trophy head ***2.*** Jack Russell sculpture ***3.*** Half scale Highland Cow head

3

www.linck.ch

Linck Keramik

A Swiss heritage in craftsmanship and innovation.

Photos by Stian Foss, Pierluigi Macor, David Willen, Moritz Lang and Rita Palanikumar.

Linck Keramik was founded in 1942 by artist Margrit Linck in Bern, Switzerland and is the result of an idea, developed over decades and generations.

Margrit Linck found inspiration when travelling to Berlin and Paris, becoming part of an emerging art scene with illustrious names such as Picasso, Giacometti and Braque. Back in Switzerland Margrit Linck realized her calling. She utilized the expertise of pottery tradition for her artistic expression. Together with surrealist art objects she began to develop a new design language and form for ceramics.

Between the 1940s and 80s Margrit Linck created hundreds of ceramic objects – over time increasingly in white. She found a simple explanation for this."I love white – since the form is of utmost importance to me, it seems that the perfect form can only come in white."

Today the potters follow traditional techniques in creating the unmistakable trademark designs by Margrit Linck – each manufactured entirely by hand on traditional potter's wheels. This lends each piece its individual character with instant recognition of the Linck Keramik aesthetic.

Since 2011, its third generation owner, Annet Berger, is committed to preserve these specialized manufacturing techniques and leading Linck Keramik into the future.

Linck Keramik fue fundada en 1942 en Berna (Suiza) por la artista Margrit Linck y es el resultado de una idea engendrada durante décadas y generaciones.

Margrit Linck encontró la inspiración viajando a Berlín y París, dónde formó parte de un escenario artístico emergente con nombres destacados como Picasso, Giacometti y Braque. Al volver a Suiza, Margrit Linck se dio cuenta de su vocación. Y así, aplicó la experiencia de la tradición alfarera a su expresión artística. Además de objetos artísticos surrealistas, comenzó a desarrollar un nuevo lenguaje de diseño y formas cerámicas.

Entre los años 40 y los años 80, Margrit Linck creó cientos de objetos en cerámica, cada vez más en blanco. Encontró una explicación sencilla para esto: "Me encanta el blanco y doy especial importancia a la forma, así que creo que la forma perfecta sólo se puede alcanzar en blanco".

En la actualidad, los alfareros siguen técnicas tradicionales para crear los inconfundibles diseños de marca de Margrit Linck, todos ellos hechos totalmente a mano en tornos tradicionales. De este modo, cada pieza cuenta con un carácter individual, aunque la estética de Linck Keramik se reconoce de inmediato.

Desde 2011, la propietaria de tercera generación, Annet Berger, está comprometida con la conservación de estas técnicas y guiar Linck Keramik hacia el futuro.

▸ V70, V52 and S256 designed in the 1970s

1

Since 2011, Annet Berger is its third generation owner.

1. Annet Berger *2.* Michael Marbach turning a S260 *3.* Stocked dry vases, waiting for pre-firing

1

2

3

4

5

6

7

Margrit Linck's love for the perfect form is pursued in the ateliers in Bern with a passion.

1. Potter's uniform ***2.*** Final touch of turning a S252 ***3.*** Preparing a bowl before assembling ***4.*** Turning on potter's wheel ***5.*** S244 waiting for the next production step ***6.*** Stocked kiln before glaze-firing ***7.*** Stored dry vases ***8.*** V94

8

1

2
5
6
3
4
7

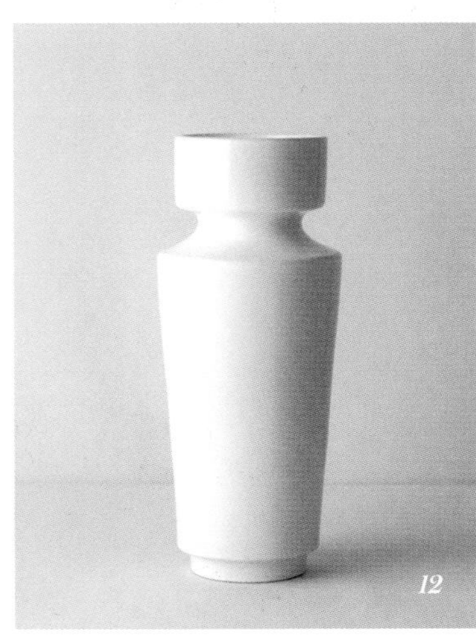

"I love white - since the form is of utmost importance to me". Margrit Linck

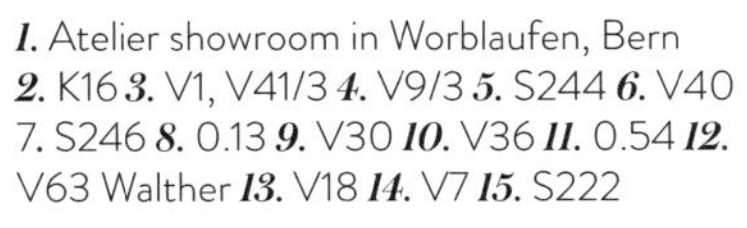

1. Atelier showroom in Worblaufen, Bern ***2.*** K16 ***3.*** V1, V41/3 ***4.*** V9/3 ***5.*** S244 ***6.*** V40 7. S246 ***8.*** 0.13 ***9.*** V30 ***10.*** V36 ***11.*** 0.54 ***12.*** V63 Walther ***13.*** V18 ***14.*** V7 ***15.*** S222

Variopinte

The Brand Variopinte developps a wear and time resistant extra flat designed dish, by using the traditional material of enamel.

Photos by Lekuonastudio and Godefroy de Virieu

The origins of Variopinte date back to 2007. For her "A Tavola" work, the designer Stefania di Petrillo decided to create a wear and time resistant extra flat designed dish, by using the traditional material of enamel.

Elevating it with a modern twist, by its shape and decoration, she adds the concept of radiant, bright and vibrant colours as only this noble material can procure.

By integrating the project with a Barzilian enameller and a Barcelona based editor, the Variopinte brand was born.

Over the season, the team developed more shapes, the collection is enriched with new colours and gives place of pride to the combinations of these models, bringing forth a concept unique in the design market for culinary and catering design.

Variopinte is used by a good number of restaurants and hotels around the world, available in store and visible in their showroom, at the same time offering a showcase and meeting place for many discoveries in Barcelona.

Los orígenes de Variopinte se remontan a 2007. Para su obra "A Tavola", la diseñadora Stefania di Petrillo decidió crear un plato de diseño extraplano resistente al tiempo y al uso, utilizando un material tradicional, el esmalte.

Dándole un giro moderno, en su forma y decoración, añadió el concepto de colores radiantes, brillantes y llamativos que sólo este material puede ofrecer.

Integrando en el proyecto a un esmaltador brasileño y un editor afincado en Barcelona, nació la marca Variopinte.

El equipo desarrolló más formas, se añadieron colores a la colección y la combinación de modelos se ubicó en un lugar privilegiado, dando lugar a un concepto único en el mercado del diseño para el sector culinario y.de catering.

Variopinte está presente en un gran número de restaurantes y hoteles de todo el mundo, disponible en su tienda y en su showroom, al mismo tiempo que ofrece un escaparate y lugar de encuentro para muchos descubrimientos en Barcelona.

▸ Variopinte products (Photo by Lekuonastudio)

Traditional material of enamel with a modern twist.

1. Stefania di Petrillo (Photo by Godefroy de Virieu) ***2.*** The showroom of the Brand in Barcelona (by Lekuonastudio) ***3.*** Combination of bowls and plates (by Lekuonastudio)
4. Products are multi use (by Lekuonastudio)

Annemarie O'Sullivan

Annemarie is a basket maker, working on small-scale domestic objects to large-scale architectural installations.

Photos by Alun Callender, Jo Crowther and Susan Bell

Annemarie is a basket maker, working on small-scale domestic objects to large-scale architectural installations. Using willow, which she grows and harvests herself, she uses weaving and binding techniques, which have been used for hundreds of years to make a range of functional and non-functional work. Annemarie is really interested in seeing the process of making through, from the source to the finished piece. Collaboration is a key part of her work. She loves to share ideas with makers from other disciplines. She likes to work in a playful way, but the end product always has a high level of craft.

She is very grateful to all the makers who came before her, who discovered amazing ways to make and construct. Without them she feels that she would have nothing. Annemarie loves the simplicity of basket making. All she needs is a knife and some rods of willow and she can make a basket.

Annemarie es una cestera que trabaja desde objetos domésticos a pequeña escala hasta grandes instalaciones arquitectónicas. Empleando sauce, que cultiva y recolecta ella misma, aplica técnicas de tejido y unión utilizadas durante cientos de años para elaborar obras tanto funcionales como no funcionales. Annemarie está muy interesada en observar el proceso, desde la materia prima hasta la pieza acabada. La colaboración es una parte fundamental de su trabajo. Le encanta compartir ideas con expertos de otras disciplinas. Le apasiona trabajar de manera alegre, aunque el producto final siempre tiene un alto nivel de elaboración.

Se siente muy agradecida con los creadores anteriores por descubrir formas increíbles de trabajar y construir. Considera que sin ellos, no tendría nada. Annemarie adora la simplicidad de la cestería. Todo lo que necesita para hacer una cesta es un cuchillo y unas varas de sauce.

▸ Annemarie's Kindling basket (Photo by Jo Crowther)

1

2

4

She uses weaving and binding techniques, which have been used for hundreds of years.

1. Annemarie O'Sullivan in her studio (Photo by Alun Callender) ***2.*** Square to round baskets (by Jo Crowther) ***3.*** Square family installation (by Jo Crowther) ***4.*** Kindling basket detail (by Jo Crowther) ***5.*** Sweet Chestnut tray detail (by Susan Bell)

3

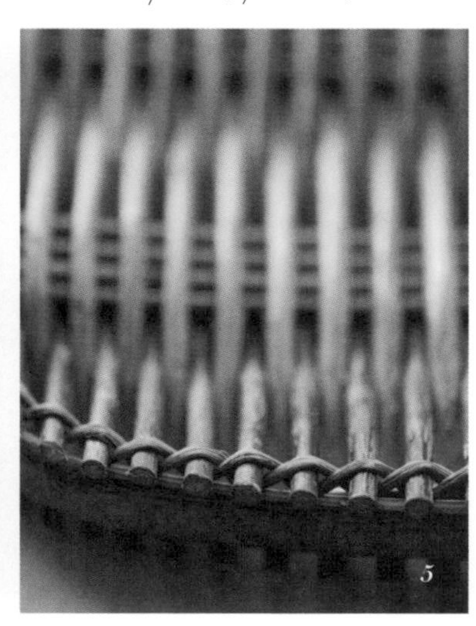

5

PETER
KIM
RENE
MARTINE

www.papabubble.com

Papabubble

The magic of the ancient artisanal candy making process.

Papabubble is an extraordinary Company where everyone's dreams can become a piece of candy. Based in Barcelona since 2004, their goal is to recover the magic of the ancient artisanal candy making process. Their philosophy is to deliver a unique experience…in every piece of Candy. New flavor, new ideas, new textures. At Papabubble they aim to surprise you every day. Their secret consists of a perfect match of Creativity + Quality + Passion

Their goal is to offer an exciting experience for all 5 of your senses with the smell of melted sugar, the bright colors of the candy, and the sweet, delicious tastes.

At Papabubble you will find their signature candy rings, candy flowers, sushi candy and the most incredible variety of lollipops. They are also able to personalize candy with names, company brands, corporate logos, along with your favorite combinations of flavors and colors. Their stores … Papabubble around the world.

They produce their handmade candies one by one with great care and dexterity. Papabubble has not invented the candy, but has reinterpreted the process adapting to changing times.

They have replaced machines with their hands in a 100% manual process that requires great skill from their master candy makers. Production takes place in view of your visitors, who can witness the entire process, smell, fee and sample the candy. A unique and unforgettable experience.

Papabubble es una compañía extraordinaria donde el sueño de cada uno se puede convertir en caramelo. Con sede en Barcelona desde 2004, su objetivo es recuperar la magia del proceso de elaboración del caramelo artesanal. Su filosofía es ofrecer una experiencia única... con cada caramelo. Nuevos sabores, nuevas ideas, nuevas texturas. En Papabubble quieren sorprender cada día. Su secreto consiste en una combinación perfecta de creatividad+calidad+pasión.

Su objetivo es ofrecer una experiencia emocionante para los cinco sentidos a través del olor del azúcar fundida, los colores brillantes del caramelo y sus dulces y deliciosos sabores.

En Papabubble hay sus caramelos redondos habituales, flores de caramelo, sushi de caramelo y la más increíble variedad de piruletas. Además, personalizan caramelos con su nombre, marca o logotipo empresarial en su combinación favorita de sabores y colores. Sus tiendas… Papabubble en todo el mundo.

Sus caramelos son elaborados a mano uno a uno con cariño y destreza. Papabubble no inventó el caramelo, pero ha reinterpretado el proceso para adaptarlo a los nuevos tiempos.

Han sustituido las máquinas por sus manos para implementar un proceso 100% manual que requiere grandes aptitudes por parte de los maestros elaboradores. La producción tiene lugar a la vista, se puede ver todo el proceso, oler, sentir y degustar los caramelos. Una experiencia única e inolvidable.

▸ Papabubble candy

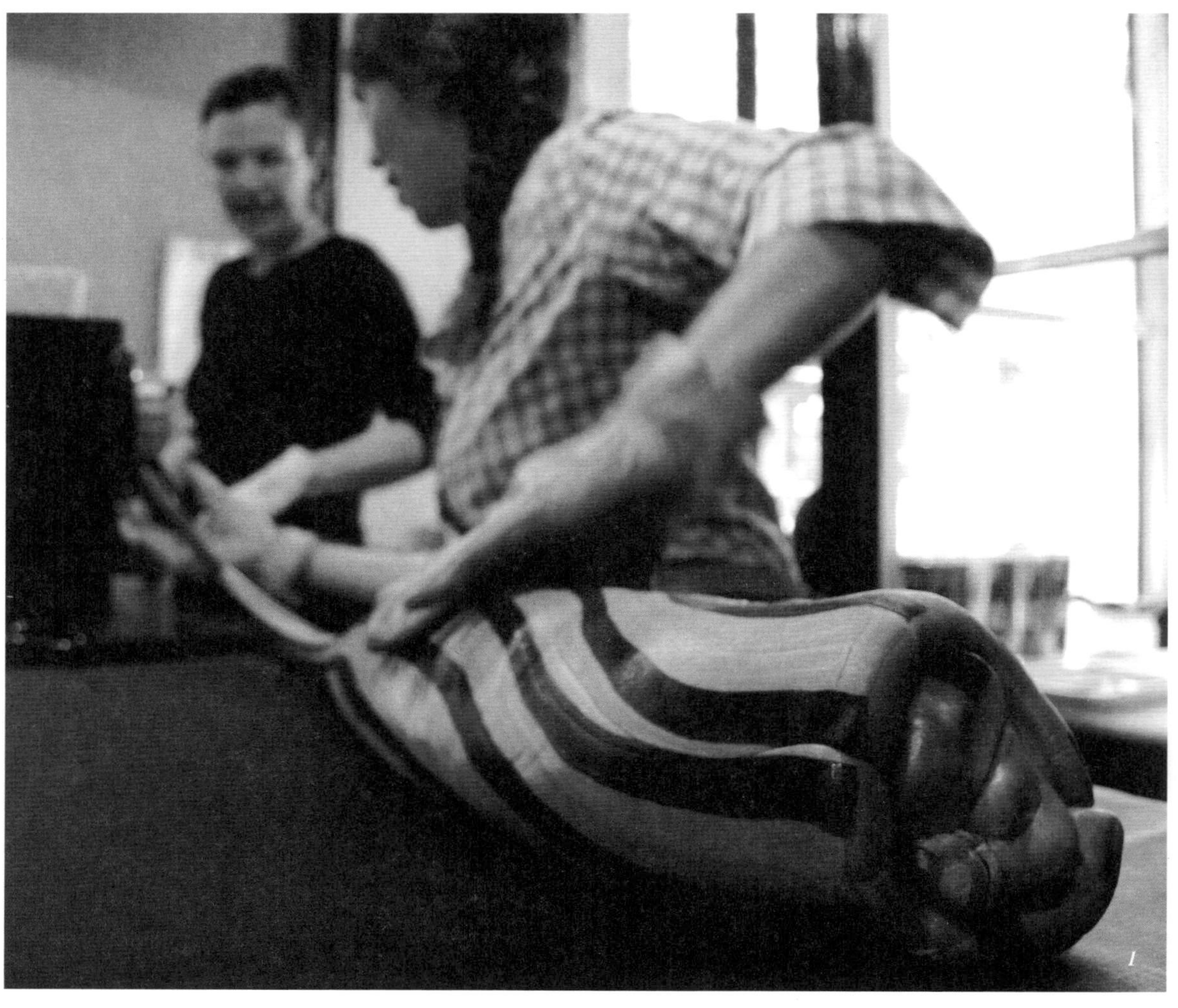

1

2

3

Papabubble has not invented the candy, but has reinterpreted the process adapting to changing times.

1. Making pillow candy *2.* Papabubble secret formula *3.* Stretching an orange *4.* #1 flavor: fruit mix *5.* The shop in Barcelona *6.* Find the logo inside *7.* Colorful candy

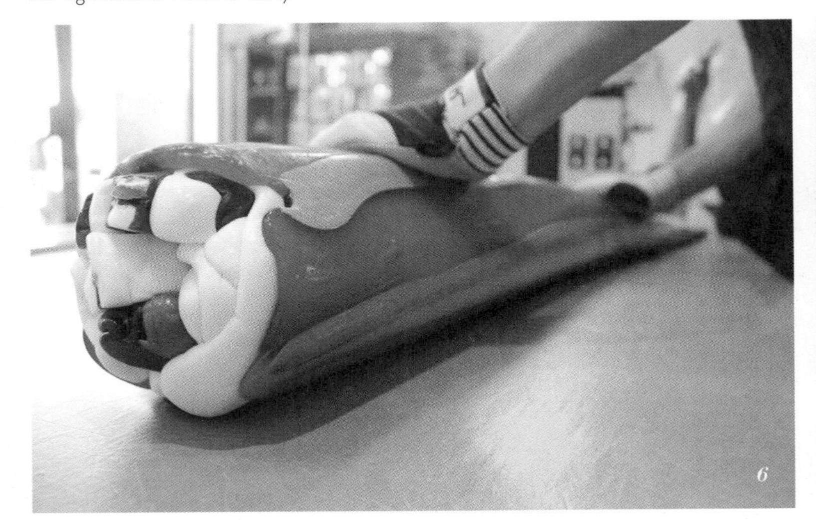
6

7

Dick Taylor
CRAFT CHOCOLATE

Dick Taylor chocolate

Adam Dick & Dustin Taylor - Chocolate Makers.

Deeply rooted in a background of woodworking and boat building, Adam & Dustin have always loved working with their hands. The concept of craft has been a guiding principle in their lives from the beginning. After hearing about what was going on in the young and growing American craft chocolate movement, they were drawn to the common threads they saw in working with wood and crafting chocolate from the bean. They became fascinated with a new challenge and loved the idea of reinventing the chocolate experience. In 2010 they bought some small scale equipment and began making chocolate.

As their appreciation for fine chocolate grew, they became increasingly attracted to blending a traditional old world European approach with a more modern take on processing. They looked far and wide for machines that could produce the level of sophistication they were looking for on a small batch scale. Alongside exceptional processing, they felt that the truest expression of the cocoa beans was to make chocolate using ONLY two ingredients; cacao and cane sugar. Simple ingredients and careful control of the entire process allows them to highlight the wonderful flavor varieties of beans from around the world. When they find excellence, they pay premiums to the farmers who do exceptional work with superb harvest and post- harvest practices. Adam & Dustin take great care in their process to build on this foundational work, allowing people to taste an elegant and refined chocolate that reflects it's origin.

Con raíces y trayectoria en la carpintería y en la construcción de barcos, a Adam & Dustin siempre les ha encantado trabajar con las manos. El concepto de artesanía ha sido un principio conductor en sus vidas desde los inicios. Tras escuchar lo que estaba pasando con el joven y creciente movimiento del chocolate artesanal americano, les atrajo el denominador común entre trabajar con la madera y elaborar chocolate desde el grano. Fascinados por el nuevo desafío, les apasionó la idea de reinventar la experiencia del chocolate. En 2010 se hicieron con un equipo a pequeña escala y comenzaron a elaborar chocolate.

A medida que creció su reconocimiento por el chocolate de calidad, les atrajo mas la combinación de un enfoque tradicional del mundo europeo y procesos más modernos. Así, buscaron , a lo largo y a lo ancho, maquinaria que pudiera producir el nivel de sofisticación que deseaban a pequeña escala. Además de a través de un proceso excepcional, consideran que la expresión verdadera del grano de cacao se alcanza elaborando chocolate con SÓLO dos ingredientes, cacao y azúcar de caña. Unos ingredientes simples y un cuidadoso control de la totalidad del proceso les permiten resaltar las maravillosas variedades de sabor de granos de todo el mundo. Cuando alcanzan la excelencia, pagan primas a los agricultores, que realizan un trabajo excepcional, empleando durante y tras la recogida, prácticas de primer nivel. Adam & Dustin cuidan mucho el proceso, permitiendo al cliente degustar un chocolate elegante y refinado que refleja su origen.

▸ 72% Belize, Toledo dark chocolate bar

Dick • Taylor
CRAFT CHOCOLA
1

Dick • Taylor
CRAFT CHOCOLATE
101
2

3

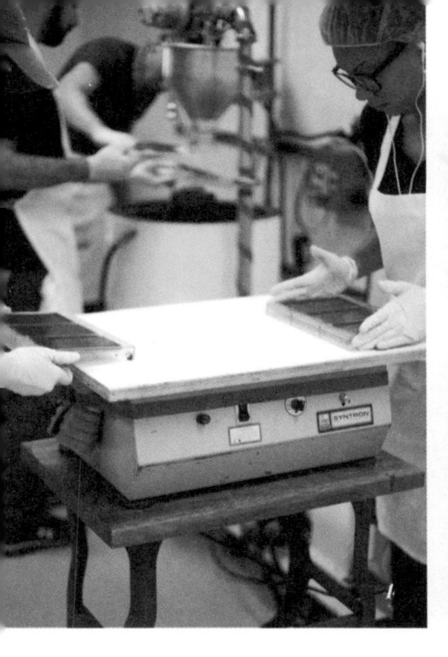

"All of our chocolate is made in our factory in northern California."

1. Adam Dick & Dustin Taylor *2.* The shop *3.* Royal #5 Bean Roaster *4.* Molding room vibrating table. Helps to eliminate air bubbles in the chocolate bar mold *5.* Owner Adam Dick hand dipping confections *6.* Inside the shop *7.* Their letter pressed packaging

aoobarcelona.com
www.marcmorro.com

AOO

AOO offers its own collection of furniture and also its creative services in commissioned furniture.

Photos by Coke Bartrina, Silvia Conde and Yosigo

AOO is a small furniture company from Barcelona established in 2013 by Oriol Villar and Marc Morro. They like things made here*, it's what makes more sense for them; sometimes made by themselves, by artisans or by local manufacturers.

Wood is mostly the starting point of their pieces, for some reasons: its smell, its warmth, its human scale to work with, but above all because wood is the most variable and adaptable raw material available to man in nature.

AOO offers its own collection of furniture and also its creative services in commissioned furniture, always with the aim of making ordinary, functional, anonymous and everyday furniture.

AOO es una pequeña compañía de muebles de Barcelona fundada en 2013 por Oriol Villar y Marc Morro. Les gustan las cosas hechas aquí*; en ocasiones son ellos mismos quienes hacen sus objetos, otras veces son realizados por artesanos o fabricantes locales.

La madera es el punto de partida de sus piezas, por varias razones: su olor, su calidez, su escala humana a la hora de trabajar, pero sobre todo porque la madera es la materia prima más variable y adaptable que la naturaleza ofrece al hombre.

AOO ofrece su propia colección de muebles, además de servicios creativos para muebles por encargo, siempre con el objetivo de crear muebles cotidianos, anónimos, funcionales y ordinarios.

▸ Toro stool

1

2

3

Making ordinary, functional, anonymous and everyday furniture.

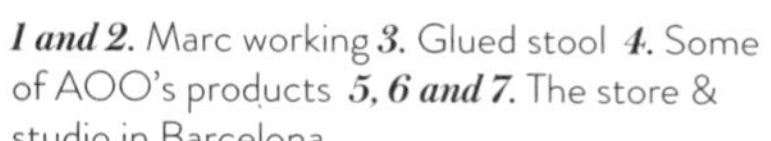

1 and 2. Marc working ***3.*** Glued stool ***4.*** Some of AOO's products ***5, 6 and 7.*** The store & studio in Barcelona